holy
play

Also by Kirk Byron Jones

Rest in the Storm: Self-Care Strategies for Clergy and Other Caregivers (Judson Press, 2001)

Addicted to Hurry: Spiritual Strategies for Slowing Down (Judson Press, 2003)

The Jazz of Preaching: How to Preach with Great Freedom and Joy (Abingdon Press, 2004)

Morning B.R.E.W.: A Divine Power Drink for Your Soul (Augsburg, 2005)

The Morning B.R.E.W. Journal (Augsburg, 2005)

The African American Preaching Library (Editor) (Abingdon Press, 2006)

holy
play

The Joyful Adventure
of Unleashing
Your Divine
Purpose

Kirk Byron Jones

JB JOSSEY-BASS

Published by Jossey-Bass
A Wiley Imprint
989 Market Street, San Francisco, CA 94103-1741   www.josseybass.com

All scripture quotations, unless otherwise indicated, are taken from the HOLY BIBLE, NEW INTERNATIONAL VERSION®. NIV®. Copyright © 1973, 1978, 1984 by International Bible Society. Used by permission of Zondervan. All rights reserved.

Readers should be aware that Internet Web sites offered as citations and/or sources for further information may have changed or disappeared between the time this was written and when it is read.

Jossey-Bass books and products are available through most bookstores. To contact Jossey-Bass directly call our Customer Care Department within the U.S. at 800-956-7739, outside the U.S. at 317-572-3986, or fax 317-572-4002.

Jossey-Bass also publishes its books in a variety of electronic formats. Some content that appears in print may not be available in electronic books.

Library of Congress Cataloging-in-Publication Data
Jones, Kirk Byron.
Holy play: the joyful adventure of unleashing your divine purpose / Kirk Byron Jones.
    p. cm.
Includes bibliographical references (p. 181) and index.
ISBN-13: 978-0-7879-8452-6 (cloth)
ISBN-10: 0-7879-8452-3 (cloth)
    1. Vocation—Christianity. 2. Dreams—Religious aspects—Christianity. 3. Christian life. I. Title.
    BV4740.J65 2007
    248.4—dc22   2006032158

Printed in the United States of America
FIRST EDITION
HB Printing   10 9 8 7 6 5 4 3 2

contents

Preface   ix

Acknowledgments   xv

1
The Tyranny and Triumph of Choosing   1

2
The Anatomy of Stuckness   15

3
The Divine Adventure   31

4
Our Great Beloved Partner   42

5
The Wild Thrill of Wide-Open Possibility   65

6
Not Just Creature but Creator   99

7
Three Great Creative Powers   120

8
Dreaming Your Way to Purpose   139

9
Joyfully Playing Your Dreams   162

Notes   181

The Author   185

Index   187

To my children and godchild:
Jasmine, Jared, Joya,
Jovonna, and Yulanda.
Thank you for keeping the play in me!

I come that they may have life, and have it
more abundantly.
JOHN 10:10

The Spirit gives life.
2 CORINTHIANS 3:6

The glory of God is a person fully alive.
IRENAEUS

Life is either a daring adventure or nothing. To keep
our faces toward change and behave like free spirits
in the presence of fate is strength undefeatable.
HELEN KELLER

The origins of play are obscure. It had a relative in
Middle Dutch *pleien* "dance about, jump for joy," but
this has now died out, leaving it in splendid but
puzzling isolation, its ancestry unaccounted for.
JOHN AYTO

The most delightful—and revolutionary—action
of all is play.
KIRK BYRON JONES

preface

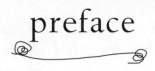

How ready are you to think of something
unfamiliar?

ANTHONY DE MELLO

Jesus asked what sounds like a cruel question one day.
He asked a man who had been lame from birth if he
wanted to be well. What a thing to ask! Oh, it sounds
better in Old English, "Wouldst thou be made whole?" But
the impact is the same. Jesus asked the man a question for
which the answer was starkly obvious. The answer was made
even more obvious by the fact that the man had taken up residence at a place known for healing. He was living beside a
pool where, allegedly, miraculous healings took place regularly. His problem, as he related to the insensitive stranger,
was that he didn't have anyone to take him to the pool. What
do you mean, Jesus, does he want to be well? Look how long
he's been unable to walk! Look where he is! Why would you
ask such a thing?

Well, it turns out that Jesus knew more about the man
than he initially let on—and even more about how authentic change takes place. Real change begins in our minds,
with our perception of reality. Jesus knew that healing was
in the vicinity; he wanted to know if the man's mind-set,
his perception, could accommodate the extraordinary

breakthrough that was about to occur. Changing your perception is like unlocking a huge vault bearing the contents of extraordinary new imaginings and possibilities.

This is a book that challenges you to change some of your most cherished beliefs and perceptions about God and purpose. Though I am a Christian writing primarily to Christians, my hope is that my words will resonate with the wider religious and spiritual audience.

Beliefs, perceptions, thoughts—our mental interpretation of life and experience—are more important than actuality. That is to say, what you think about something matters more than the something itself, because what you think, as far as you are concerned, is that something. Our interpretation of reality is the true reality. If I show you a red shoe and no matter what I tell you, you are convinced that the shoe is green, it doesn't matter that it is actually red. The shoe is green to you. The green shoe is your perception, your belief, and thus your experience of that moment. What's most important in life is the way we perceive life, what we believe about life. We construct life experience with the stuff of our beliefs and perceptions, those we manufacture on our own and those we receive from others. As we think, so we are.

Our challenge and one that we pay too little attention to in the haste and overload of modern life is to regularly attend to our thoughts. We create undue suffering and hardship in every dimension of living because of the way we think about things and continue to think about things. Tending to our thoughts—excavating, examining, destroying, and creating them—takes time, energy, and focus. We are often low on all three simultaneously.

Be that as it may, I challenge you to give more attention to what you believe and to changing your beliefs in the areas of your most sustained discomfort. Changing your perception unleashes creative energy that empowers you to change your behavior and change your condition. Change your perspective, and you change your experience.

Unfortunately, once we have identified ideas and beliefs that do more harm than good, we are often reluctant to change them. If changing our thoughts can result in amazing positive transformations, why do we so vigorously resist changing what we believe about things?

There are many reasons. We grow overly comfortable with what is familiar to us and cling to it even when it no longer of value. There is the story about the woman always cut off two large slices of a ham before baking it. When she was asked why she did this, she responded, "That's how my mother always did it." When the mother was finally asked why she always cut off two slices of ham, she explained, "I didn't have a pot big enough to fit a whole ham." Yet the daughter continued to remove two slices. Often we hold on to what we think for no good reason other than familiarity. This overcomfortability with the familiar is linked to our fear of the unknown and to what Anthony De Mello more perceptively diagnosed as "our fear of the loss of the known," and it keeps us in deadening sameness.

Safety is another reason for thinking the same things. If a child believes that a night light helps ward off unwelcome mysterious ghostly intruders and draws solace from that perception, altering that belief is almost impossible. Similarly, persons opposed to racial integration in the United States in the 1960s held on to their prejudices and biases in part because of the safety it offered from encountering persons who were different.

Old beliefs provide perceived benefits that we are unwilling to relinquish. My teenage and younger daughters, when getting into the car, still call out the right to ride in the front seat: "I've got the front seat!" They believe that there is something about being up front that offers a better riding experience. Maybe it's the idea that one can see more. Of course, if the ride is perceived as an opportunity to focus on reading, listening to music, or talking, then a case can be made for the back seat as offering the more favorable space.

Sometimes beliefs are grasped tightly because of the company they allow us to keep. We may accept something as true because it is the accepted truth of persons we appreciate being linked to. To believe something new would pose a great risk to continued community with those we love and respect.

We may resist exchanging one idea for another due to the tension associated with such a transaction. As Martin Luther King Jr. railed against racism and segregation in Birmingham during the civil rights movement, he was asked by well-meaning clergy to stifle his efforts in the spirit of peace. They interpreted the tension created by the advent of social change as not being in the best interest of the body politic. In his now legendary "Letter from Birmingham Jail," King reminded his colleagues that "creative tension" was necessary for positive change to take place.

There is another formidable reason why daring to think different thoughts about God—this book's challenge to you—may be difficult at first. It is possible that in our minds, our thoughts about God are indistinguishable from what we understand to be God. Thus we surmise, perhaps more unconsciously than consciously, that "to change my cherished deeply held beliefs about God is to change God. I don't dare attempt such a thing. What could be more sinful?" The fact is that God and our views of God are two different things. When it comes to God, all thought falls short; wouldn't you agree? I would argue that if our views about God are not in constant faithful flux, our perception of God is too small.

In the following pages, I will ask you to reconsider your views about God, especially views related to human aspiration and vocation. I will argue that much of our cherished traditional theological thinking is in fact blocking our capacity to live adventurously and creatively. Narrow thinking about God leads to heartbreakingly thin imagination and ingenuity. Commonly accepted views about God as producer, writer, director, and main actor in our lives promotes a robotic existence in which living God's will is often perceived as being diametrically opposed to following one's deepest yearnings. Moreover, traditional beliefs have grown unnecessary confusions and inhibitions, weeds that have sapped all the creativeness right out of life for many of the well-meaning faithful. This plight is just plain unacceptable, not to mention unholy. Because of their usually deep entrenchment and perceived untouchableness, there is nothing more hideous than spiritual perspectives that have the effect of diminishing life in unsuspecting ways. The most dangerous beliefs are the ones we don't think to question.

In my wildest mood, my goal for this book is to blow the top off our understandings of God and life's purpose that hold us down instead of setting us free. Where purpose is concerned, I believe that God's ultimate will for all of us is to play and soar in excited freedom and holy abandonment. Playing and soaring, that's right. Living your purpose more freely and expansively causes your heart—and God's—to sing. Are you feeling confused and frustrated about your purpose even after reading detailed books that guarantee direct access to divine will? Your purpose is not a mysterious code to be painstakingly broken and deciphered. Purpose is an open invitation from God to playfully (joyfully and creatively) imagine and live your boldest dreams. This book will teach you how to stop waiting for God to tell you what to do and start confidently doing what God has been inspiring you to do all along. Get ready to be free to move forward with your life in exciting new ways. Prepare to engage the joyful adventure of unleashing your divine purpose.

acknowledgments

I am deeply grateful to all persons who knowingly and unknowingly brought this book to life. That having been said, I am especially grateful for those of you who knew full well what you were doing:

To Sarah Jane Freymann, my agent, for believing in me and having the skill and patience to bring greater clarity and focus to ideas bumping into each other inside me. You are a wonder!

To Sheryl Fullerton, executive editor at Jossey-Bass, for your graceful precision with the first draft and thoughtful advice throughout. Your March 1, 2006, letter shall remain with me as a ready guide for "playing with fire," ordinarily referred to as writing.

To everyone at Jossey-Bass who contributed to *Holy Play* in any way, especially Joanne Clapp Fullagar and Catherine Craddock.

To Shari Lynne Smothers, a dear friend and a wonderful poet (read *Pebbles in My Shoes*), for listening to and calling forth new ideas.

To Markeithia Lavon Silver, my sister by loving choice if not by birth, for her boldness and intellectual and spiritual thirst.

and

To "Bunnie," my fabulous, faithful, and fun-loving spouse for over twenty-five years, and my teacher-children (they are professors to me), Jasmine, Jared, Joya, and Jovonna, for accepting the serious and celebrating the silly in me.

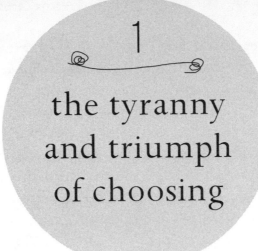

1

the tyranny and triumph of choosing

didn't know what to do. For three and a half years, I was founding pastor of Beacon Light Baptist Church in New Orleans, Louisiana, the city where I was born and grew up. I watched with humble amazement as the new congregation grew from forty members to over seven hundred, including many family members and friends. People of all walks of life found their way to 1551 Mirabeau Avenue for engaging weekly group activities and several spirited Sunday worship services.

Making my way toward the pulpit each Sunday—past persons seated in the rear hallway because the small sanctuary was filled to capacity—was like walking into the eye of a sacred ecstatic storm. Twenty-five years later, I can still see and hear the late Gwendolyn Johnson, my friend and minister of music, hammering away at the organ and belting out in her soulful alto, "I'm looking for a miracle." Following her lead, the Beacon Light Church choir and congregation would begin clapping and swaying, setting the church and their young pastor on spiritual fire. Sunday evenings, the fervor resumed with Witness Workshop, an hourlong training session in which persons learned how to communicate their faith in courteous ways in their homes, work settings, and public places. The day climaxed with Sunday Night Live, an informal evening praise celebration that held an extra element of sacred surprise. The worship was less structured, allowing for greater spontaneity and freedom of expression.

In the middle of this stirring and wondrous experience, I was thinking about resigning. I felt full and hungry at the same time. While coming home to pastor had been a spiritual adventure beyond my boldest imaginings, a compelling new desire to teach in a seminary began welling up inside me. In order to fully meet the requirements of the new vision, I felt I needed to earn a Ph.D. in a discipline (Christian social ethics) and in a setting that New Orleans did not provide. Therein was my conflict: Should I remain in New Orleans as pastor of a dynamic church or resign to pursue further theological study that would prepare me for a seminary teaching career?

At first, I thought about continuing as pastor and commuting to the school of my choice. But stubborn questions grabbed me and would not turn me loose: "Can you hold both flames at the same time?" "Can you manage a thriving church and a rigorous academic program simultaneously?" "If you do this, what time will you have left to be a caring husband and father?" "OK," I concluded, "I'll take a sabbatical, a leave of absence, to at least begin the academic program. That way, I won't have to leave the church entirely. Once I am done, I'll return to my full responsibilities as pastor." In quieter moments, the not-so-subtle dishonesty of that solution haunted me. I could not honestly tell the members of Beacon Light Church that I would return after my Ph.D. program had commenced or was completed because I was not certain that I would return.

"What should I do?" On the surface of things, it didn't make sense to even contemplate leaving. What pastor gives up a growing congregation that, moreover, just happens to be located where he was born? Though it made sense in my mind, choosing to remain where I was did not bring peace to my heart. Deeply divided and weighted down with decision fatigue, I traveled to a religious conference in Poughkeepsie, New York. Although I do not remember a single event associated with the conference, I will never forget a spiritual encounter on the banks of the Hudson River.

The Breakthrough

It was Sunday morning; my congregation, I imagined, was having a time of high praise while I was hundreds of miles away attending a clergy meeting. During the gathering, I

walked out of one of the sessions to hold a meeting of my
own: a conference with God. This would be a deeply honest talk in which I would hold nothing back, including my
frustration. That's right. God would tell me right then and
there why I had been placed in such a bind, why I was
being forced to choose between a great blessing and a great
desire. And oh, yes, the meeting would not end until God
told me clearly what choice to make regarding my future.

I met with God on the banks of the Hudson River. I
walked to a spot and began to silently voice my confusion
and consternation. I remember, in the words of the gospel
song of total surrender, laying it "all on the altar." After a
while, I stopped speaking, bowed my head, closed my eyes,
and just stood still. My prayer became a posture of quiet
waiting. Having talked myself empty, I just stood there.

Some moments passed, and I finally opened my eyes.
For the first time since coming to the riverbank, I noticed
my surroundings; that's when I saw them: two paths, just
below where I was standing. I held them in view for as long
as it took these words to sound in my soul: "Know this:
Whichever path you choose, I will be with you."

I heard the words clearly and distinctly, as if I had
heard an audible voice, though I had not. The mysterious
promise, "Know this: Whichever path you choose, I will be
with you," seemed to instantly melt the tension surrounding my decision. I felt the anxiety and stress that had accu-
mulated over the prior weeks and months beginning to
leave my body. A strange but welcome peaceful empowerment took their place. I couldn't make sense of all I was

feeling, but I knew something significant was happening; something was changing.

Somehow, sensing the deep and lasting meaning of the moment, I wanted something to remind me that what had happened to me had really happened. Looking down, I picked up a small stick lying on the ground and placed it in my shirt pocket. The stick would be my point of continuing contact with the surprising promise: "Know this: Whichever path you choose, I will be with you." I have kept this 3½-inch-long scrap of wood for over two decades now. Whenever I hold it, it reminds me of the promise on the banks of the Hudson River.

The Meaning of the Mysterious Promise

Until my encounter in upstate New York, I believed that vocational decision making was a matter of discerning and following God's preordained plan for one's life. Perhaps most of you reading this book grew up with a similar belief. It is a belief fed, in part, by biblical stories of persons who seemed to have had their destinies drawn up in full for them by God: Moses, Jeremiah, Mary, and Jesus. In Jeremiah's case, the call on his life is made prior to his birth:

> Before I formed you in the womb I knew you,
> and before you were born I consecrated
> you; I appointed you a prophet to the nations.

Jeremiah 1:5 (NRSV)

Many of us have universalized this understanding of predetermined divine appointment. Not only are *some* persons
called to fulfill certain life quests, even before they are born,
but *all* of us are. Thus the goal of vocational discernment is
to decipher the divine calling already inside you. If you are
having trouble seeing what God has called you to do, all
you have to do is look harder, or "get right with God."

For me, discerning and heeding God's call meant
entering the ministry as a teenager. Family and church
members confirmed my life mission by supporting me
with prayers, encouraging words, and finances as I learned
the essential tasks of ministry. Through high school, college,
seminary, and my first full-time pastorate, I had no reason
to doubt that I was doing the work God wanted me to do.
I intended to follow God's plan as I best I could. Things
went smoothly until my dilemma about leaving a pastorate
I loved. As I had done with other decisions in my life, I
prayed and waited for God to show me the way, to reveal
the next place on the map that was my life plan. When God
finally spoke, I heard something different and fresh which
eventually led me to radically alter my thinking about vocational discernment as predetermined divine appointment.

Challenging Divine Appointment

The new liberating idea that hit me with a jolt on the
Hudson River was that vocation is not solely God's choice;
it is *my* choice. Thinking that vocational decision making

was only a matter of discovering what God had already decided for me created tragic unintended results.

First, it resulted in my dis-tancing myself from genuine desires and longings, reali-ties that were (and are) some of God's best gifts to me (and you). As much as I loved preach-ing and serving God's people as a pastor, I was engulfed by a consuming pas-sion for learning more and teach-ing. Reading, questioning, and pondering had the power to absorb me like few other things in my life. (Anything that overtakes you so ought never be taken lightly.) Yet as I strug-gled to decide between pastoring and continuing my edu-cation, I found myself at times blocking my desires and belittling my longings. A mind-set that pits earnest desire against God's will needs to be challenged. I believe that observing a vital connection between God's will and our earnest desires has the power to revolutionize our thinking about vocation and work choices for the better.

Another result of believing that vocation was just a matter of living a prewritten script was feeling more fear than thrill for the sacred transition building inside me. Instead of being excited by a new dawning, I tormented myself: "What if I make the wrong choice? What if I miss God's will for my life? What if I blow it?" Why would a

> The new liberating idea that hit me with a jolt was that vocation is not solely God's choice; it is *my* choice.

> A mind-set that pits earnest desire against God's will needs to be challenged.

loving and gracious God make vocational discernment such a gruesome and painful affair? The answer is that God does not; we do with our overly narrow understanding of vocational choice making. Being free to assume more responsibility for our life's choices, including vocational ones, frees us to take more joy regarding them. Not fully celebrating our blessed right to make choices is the worst choice of all—and perhaps the one choice that grieves God the most.

"Know this: Whichever path you choose, I will be with you" granted me unexpected permission to choose my way without fear. Throughout my discerning process, one fear loomed larger than any other: the fear of making the wrong choice, one that would divert me from the "divinely ordained plan for my life." It was refreshing relief to know that neither of my choices would be "wrong" in God's eyes. This knowledge empowered me to make my own decision about what I wanted to do. It challenged me to believe that faithfulness was less about *surrendering* and more about *assuming responsibility* for my life. Put another way, it prompted me to interpret faithfulness to God not just in terms of submission to divine authority but also in terms of embracing the divine empowerment already in me.

A third unintended result of thinking that vocation was a matter of decoding a divine prewritten script was believing that the best vocational choice is always a singular choice. In my own mind, I was trying to determine which road would be the best for me, continuing to pastor or pursing a Ph.D. It had not dawned on me that my way of formulating the equation was problematic. I envisioned there having to be a best and less than best solution. The riverbank promise opened my eyes and mind to the prospect of a *broadened best*, a way of interpreting "best" in pluralistic rather than singular terms. What if any number of roads could be the "best" for me, equally blessed and condoned by God? Since that revelation, I have beheld the lavish diversity of nature countless times and wondered how any of us can be duped into holding on to narrow, confined, singular notions of "best."

The fourth unintended result of believing that vocational expression is a matter of living according to God's ordered plan is to feel stuck when that plan is not readily apparent. What do you do when you want to do what God wants you to do but you just don't know what that is? If your earnest desire is to please and obey God, you wait. You

> What if any number of roads could be the "best" for me, equally blessed and condoned by God?

wait until God decides to tell you or the blinders are removed from your eyes. Waiting while rolling around the same thoughts over and over again leads to agonizing, if faithful, frustration. One solution is finally receiving a clear directive from God. Another is to believe a new truth: Our waiting is not the result of divine delay or human confusion but rather the consequence of human resistance to making God-inspired choices. Divine guidance is best received when we see the *dance* in *guidance* and actively play our part in the holy human adventure we call life.

What do you do when you want to do what God wants you to do but you just don't know what that is?

Losing Life-Deadening Ideas

Believing that our purpose in life is some fixed thing that we passively receive from God is deadening. Such a belief blinds us to the reality of multiple bests in life. Part of the frustration related to discerning our work has to do with wanting to be in "God's perfect will." Often that will is interpreted very narrowly. Some people think, "Though there may be several callings in life that I might want to fulfill, the one I really want is the one that God wants for me." Holding on fast and tight to this idea places us on a faithful but futile search for the "one thing" God has called me to do in life. However, is it not possible to interpret God's will in nonsingular ways? Moreover, is it not more reasonable to do so given the lavish diversity of our world and universe? What difference would it make for you to believe that there are many different tasks you can meet and roles you can fill in life? How would it make you feel to know that many of them, if not all of them, are stamped with the seal of "God's best for you"? To live our purpose more freely and enthusiastically, we must first expand our notions of "God's perfect will" and "God's best."

Another way in which the traditional understanding of purpose deadens life is that it nullifies human creativity. Why must we assume that our purposes are ready-made, especially given the Creator's issuance of dominion to humankind in the Genesis narrative of creation? We may do so out of respect for God's mysterious and omnipotent power.

I contend that we do so more because we have been taught that God wants to program us, wants to tell us what to do. I object! Stop wanting God to tell you what to do. God wants to inspire you; God does not want to control you. To want God to tell you what to do is to give back God's greatest gift to you: freedom. Close to freedom in terms of divine and wondrous gifts is the gift of our creative impulses. This gift is fresh and freely manifested in our first years. As children, we live beyond all inhibition and prohibition, to make, to create, to play, to imagine. Why wouldn't God want such primal forces to be at our disposal for designing our life's work? Why would God open us up as children to shut us down as adults? Any thought or deed that thwarts human ingenuity and creativity is not of God but rather an enemy of the truly divine. This includes the thought that God dictates a purpose for us to discover. No. We are called to join God in cocreating purpose and life itself.

God wants to inspire you; God does not want to control you.

Finally, I oppose a closed, God-domineering understanding of purpose on grounds of delight. Earlier this week, I penned a letter to be read at a loved one's funeral. In it, I said the following about Alberta Brock:

> During our stay in Chester, we grew closer. We cannot count the meals eaten, the conversations held, and perhaps most memorable of all, the moments of laughter. Her devout commitment to the faith included a pleasant disposition and a lightheartedness. We loved her smile that could come suddenly, catching you by surprise. We loved the way she laughed freely at jokes and the humor in life, including the funny things "God's people" could say and do.

Delight, joy for and in life, is a sacred gift that gets snuffed out when divining one's purpose becomes a bur-

densome and puzzling affair. Looking for God's will in a
way so narrowly configured and so unwelcoming of human
creative initiative may be "faithful," but it sure ain't fun. (I
contend that it isn't all that faithful either.)

Now, delight is a small matter if your idea of faithfulness has little room for it. I happen to believe that living
delight is at the heart of God's original and overriding purpose for all creation. One of my favorite testimonies to this
is found in Madeleine L'Engle's *Glimpses of Grace*. In an entry
called "Enjoying God," L'Engle records the conversation of
two sisters in a convent. Joaquina has become increasingly
incensed by Sister Mariana's open
appreciation for life. For her
part, Marianna does not
back down; she continues
to take joy:

> I happen to believe that living delight is at the heart of God's original and overriding purpose for all creation.

"I don't know,"
Joaquina said flatly.
She looked across the
table at Mother Escol-
astica. "I don't mean to
criticize, Mother, but there's
something wrong with it."

"With what, child?"

"The way Sister Mariana looks out the window at
the flowers, and the way she enjoys that orange."

"Well?"

"She enjoys it too much."

Mariana's mouth was full of juicy pulp. "Aren't
we supposed to?"

How do *you* answer the question "Aren't we supposed to greatly enjoy life?" If the answer is yes, that means that even our arduous struggles often give way to joy, and there is more joy to be had in any given moment than we are usually willing to see or allow ourselves to take.

Discernment is not inevitably and automatically a trying matter. One of the essential messages of holy play is that we can loosen up when it comes to purpose, see ourselves not tensely searching for it but joyfully playing and dancing it. With divine guidance? You bet—just follow the last syllable of the word *guidance*.

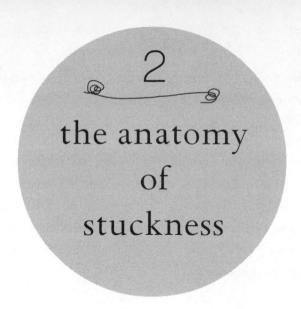

2

the anatomy
of
stuckness

Her angst was so thick, I felt like I could slice it with a knife. My friend had driven me to the airport, and we were seated at a table, talking in a restaurant. She was earnestly trying to move forward with the next vocational chapter in her life, but something was holding her back. She was clear about the things she wanted to focus on and seemed to trust her talent in those areas. As I listened to her longing, I felt that any one of the paths she had identified could provide her with a satisfying life and a comfortable wage. Nonetheless, overflowing with vision and desire, she was still stuck. Though she could see the terrain of her vision, she could not step onto its turf. Finally, I leaned across the table and asked her, "What would it take for you to move from here to there?" Thinking for just a moment, she responded, "A bridge. I need a bridge." I paused, replayed her response in my mind, and asked, "Then why don't you build one?"

Part of building a bridge between a dream and its fulfillment is coming to terms with being stuck. We must identify what it is that holds us where we are, preventing our journey to where we want to be. Because we are wired differently, come from varied backgrounds, and face unique situations, perhaps there are as many reasons for vocational stuckness as there are persons. Let's examine some common reasons for being stuck.

The Loss of the Known

In his book *Awareness*, the spiritual teacher Anthony De Mello makes a profoundly liberating distinction: "It's not that we fear the unknown. You cannot fear something that you do not know. Nobody is afraid of the unknown. What you really fear is the loss of the known."

De Mello's distinction is illustrated by a familiar (though forgotten by most of us) rite of passage: the first day of school. Many youngsters cry and cling to their parents in a valiant effort to prevent sudden change. Driven less by a new environment they have not encountered, their fear is stirred more by suddenly having to leave the things they know behind, including toys, rooms, and loved ones. What young children fear most on the first day of school is the loss of the known.

The loss of the known is a less complicated, if no less painful, affair when it is forced on us on our first day of school or five or six years earlier at birth. More trying is being in a position to actually choose to lose (and loose) the known. Making a new vocational choice is choosing to lose the known, and its primary benefits are comfort and control.

Voluntarily yielding up the known as adults is no mild concession. It means deliberately handing over some sense of certain fit in a world that is in constant flux. And it means giving up control of a setting or situation that we have tamed or that has become familiar to us. To give up the known and familiar is to give up our power of the known in exchange for the powerlessness of the unknown. One way to avoid suffering the discomfort and powerlessness of change is to get stuck, at least temporarily.

Such stuckness may be unavoidable for most of us, given the nature of our losses, but it must not become permanent. Stuckness is at best an interim place. We must stay there just long enough to develop sufficient courage to move forward toward our desired destiny.

The Tyranny of Too Many Choices

Toy shopping with our youngest child, Jovonna, used to be a grueling affair. Joyful anticipation and excitement quickly gave way to agony over which toy or toys to buy. There were times when my wife or I had to place a time limit on her because she would walk up and down the aisles over and over again picking up and putting down items. At points, she would bring us in on the process by asking for our thoughts about a toy, but we soon discovered this was just a tactic she used to buy more in-store shopping time. Jovonna was experiencing what Barry Schwartz calls "the paradox of choice":

> As the number of available choice increases, as it has in our consumer culture, the autonomy, control, and liberation this variety brings are powerful and positive. But as the number of choices keeps growing, negative aspects of having a multitude of options begin to appear. As the number of choices grows further, the negatives escalate until we become overloaded. At this point, choice no longer liberates, but debilitates. It might even be said to tyrannize.

We may adapt to too many choices by staying put. The desire and, even more, the ability to do many things well can place us in a holding pattern. The problem, in part, is having multiple options of comparable worth. It is easier to choose when choices are clearly good or bad. But what do you do when choices seem to hold equal joy-bearing potential, when opportunities (or toys) evoke roughly the same inner excitement? You do what Jovonna and many of us do: You go back and forth, trying to isolate that one distinguishing feature that will produce a clear winner, the best choice. Making this determination often means asking the same questions and coming to the same conclusions over and over again. That's when you're truly stuck.

Burnout

Sometimes stuckness may be attributed to our emotional and physical circuits having become so overloaded that we are unable to think clearly. Even if we may want to, we simply, for a time, do not seem to possess the focusing and tension-holding energy that vocational discernment requires.

Burnout is no minor, isolated experience. Many workers today feel excess stress leading to anxiety, depression, and disease.

One is led to wonder how much of our burnout is related to job frustration, to a confused and diminished sense of purpose. And how much burnout could be remedied if our heartfelt desires could also be our work? In *Crossing the Unknown Sea: Work as a Pilgrimage of Identity*, David Whyte learns that the antidote to exhaustion is not necessarily rest. "The antidote to exhaustion," he is told, "is wholeheartedness":

> You are so tired through and through because a good
> half of what you do here in this organization has
> nothing to do with your true powers, or the place

you have reached in your life. You are only half here, and half here will kill you after a while. You need something to which you can give your full power.

Thus perhaps the most effective remedy for burnout is to discover what's truly burning deeply inside of you.

Fear of Wrong Choices

I remember a popular game show from my childhood called *Let's Make a Deal*. The show was like a roller-coaster ride for contestants and viewers alike. In seconds, a big winner could become an even bigger loser. After winning something of value, the host would immediately tempt the contestant with the prospect of winning a better prize contained in an envelope, hidden under a box, or secreted behind a curtain or door. Rarely did contestants make quick and deliberate choices; most agonized. Complicating matters was the fact that size was no sure indicator of worth. Behind a curtain could be a luxurious sedan or a donkey. An envelope might contain tickets for a dream vacation or confetti. Members of the studio audience added to the excited tension of it all by screaming their preferred choices at confused contestants trying to make the right choice and trying even harder not to make the wrong choice.

I suspect that most contestants spent more time agonizing over making the wrong decision than they did pondering making the right one. "What if I'm wrong?" "What

if the deal is a bad one?" "What if I make a mistake?" These
were the questions etched on the foreheads of anxious contestants. Ultimately, they had to decide one
way or another when time ran
out. In life, we usually have
more time to make deci-
sions than the seconds
allotted in a game show.
But the extra time may
allow us to put off being
wrong indefinitely. Fear of
making the wrong choice
can keep us from making any
choice at all and from fully realizing
the promise of our dreams.

Fear of making the wrong choice can keep us from making any choice at all and from fully realizing the promise of our dreams.

Inevitability

Martin Luther King Jr. once wrote, "Human progress never
rolls in on the wheels of inevitability." He was responding
to people who advised him to slow down, delay some of his
plans for social change, and allow time for minds to change
naturally. King's response was that time had no innate, liberating, redemptive power on its own. We have to create
justice within time to make justice happen.

There are different kinds and states of waiting. "Quiet
waiting" has to do with the emptying of mind and heart of
all thoughts and sentiments in order to make room for

reflectivity and freshness. Expectant waiting, the waiting associated with, for example, the season of Advent, is filled with longing and anticipatory excitement. I don't believe King was challenging these ultimately creative forms of waiting but rather waiting that is laced with fear. That kind of waiting neither makes room for nor looks toward future events; it is locked in a fixed position. Any change will come through the passage of time and the intruding beat of inevitability. We don't change actively because it is perceived as too risky, moving us away from the way things comfortably are. Although we may feel relieved of the risks of a decision, we face an even more daunting risk: remaining stuck as time, irresponsibly perceived and experienced, passes us and our dreams by.

Waiting on God

Many of us—and I would suspect most of you reading this book—have been taught that God usually makes us wait to learn what our vocation should be. Biblical stories are often used to substantiate God's propensity toward waiting. The children of Israel toil forty years in the wilderness before entering into the Promised Land. Jacob has to wait fourteen years before being allowed to marry his beloved Rachel. Joseph serves years before rising to the upper echelon of governmental service. In the New Testament, we are told of various people who wait many years to behold the face of the anointed one, wait to receive their healing, or wait to embark on their ministries. In addition, there are the soaring poetic waiting texts of Scripture:

> They that wait on the Lord shall renew their
> strength.
> They shall mount up on wings as eagles; they shall
> run
> and not be weary, they shall walk and not faint.

Isaiah 40:31

> I waited patently on the Lord and he inclined unto
> me
> and heard my cry.

Psalm 40:1

To biblical admonitions we may also add the entire liturgical season known as Advent: a time of expectant waiting. Those of us raised in the Christian faith are taught that waiting is God's way. It is a small step, and perhaps even an inevitable one, to carry this notion of waiting into our perceptions of vocational discernment. Though waiting is an important recurring theme in Scripture, it is never trumpeted as

> Those of us raised in the Christian faith are taught that waiting is God's way.

an ideal or perpetual state. Waiting culminates in coming, in breakthrough. And the breakthrough is often sooner rather than later, sometimes surprisingly and abruptly so.

Many of the narratives in which Jesus heals has him doing so quickly and without hesitation. Moreover, there are texts that pointedly challenge the waiting posture. In Acts, early believers are challenged to get a move on, to stop standing up and gazing into the sky where Jesus has just ascended. Such stories and instances highlight the fact that the God of the Judeo-Christian faith is very much a "now" as well as a "not yet" deity.

Yet the not-yet God may be the preferred God. There are hidden benefits to believing that God has me on hold, even when I am the one doing the holding. For example, believing that God is the one holding things up frees me from the often arduous and draining effort of decision making. Moreover, believing that God has pressed the hold button yields the luxury of avoiding a mistake. Finally, everything can remain possible if I don't select "this thing" or "that thing." As it is, many people would rather live in the illusory land of grand possibilities than in the place of declared decision. For these reasons and more, the waiting

> The God of the Judeo-Christian faith is very much a "now" as well as a "not yet" deity.

we attribute to God is often less divinely inspired and more humanly contrived.

As there are hidden benefits, there are significant, often hidden difficulties with an image of the waiting God, especially as related to decision making. First, there is the problem of *mystery*. Among the things that many of us are taught about God is the belief that God is mystery. Some people argue that the best definition of God is our person- ification of mystery. The mystery dimension of God was presented to me early in life through the often communi- cated black church credo: "God is so high you can't go over Him, so wide you can't go around Him, and so low you can't go under Him."

Though I would seriously question any understanding of God that eliminated mystery, I do sense that we may have a hard time gaining clarity about decisions from an entity we ultimately believe to be mysterious. Waiting on God regarding life choices, or anything else for that matter, is an inevitable constant when God is perceived to be beyond human comprehension. If that's the case, we end up in a chronic state of not-knowing.

Another consequence of overfixating on waiting on God is what I refer to as the shadow of the selfish God. In this view, God, not sufficiently satisfied with creating humankind with free will, wishes to tell humans what to do in every instance from the cradle to the grave. This understanding of a God so involved in human affairs is hard to challenge because it is so deeply entrenched in our thinking and liturgy.

For example, a popular gospel song begs for God to "order my steps." Though the intention may be for divine companionship, the effect is often an unconscious diminished responsibility for conceptualizing and executing one's own steps, which is a part of the dance of life. I prefer the earlier hymn, "Just a Closer Walk with Thee." It affirms intimacy with the divine without nullifying human intentionality and responsibility. If it is God who ultimately orders my steps, then I may interpret standing still as God's will; my stuckness receives divine sanction.

Another problem with waiting on God is this presumption behind it: God is ever deliberating. One of the most agonizing aspects of life is waiting when it seems there is no good reason to be doing so, when we are waiting due to a lack of commitment or sensitivity on the part of others. We may become even more frustrated if we sense that we are waiting to delay action in the hope that we will be able to alter or rescind our request.

If it is God who ultimately orders my steps, then I may interpret standing still as God's will; my stuckness receives divine sanction.

Why would God make us wait? Why would God delay the realization of our aspirations and dreams? There are some plausible answers. Waiting teaches us patience and other lessons that can only be taught through the passing of time. Waiting allows for different and often more satisfying alternatives and possibilities to emerge, much like the switching of dishes in a buffet line. A few seconds can mean the difference between scraps and healthy portions.

Regardless of some benefits of waiting, when it isn't truly divinely inspired, waiting can yield less than desirable results. Here is a story I remember hearing more than one minister tell in the church of my youth, Mount Hermon Baptist Church in New Orleans:

> Once there was a man trapped in a home being engulfed by a flood. Realizing his predicament, some neighbors trudged through the waters to save him. Surprisingly, he refused their aid, saying, "The Lord will save me." Time passed, and the waters climbed higher. Suddenly, rescue workers in a boat appeared and yelled out to the man to climb aboard. But as before, he refused, saying, "The Lord will save me." Eventually, the flood forced the man to the top of his roof, where a helicopter pilot spotted him and lowered a hanging ladder. The man looked, shook his head, and shouted, "The Lord will save me." The stunned pilot hovered for as long as he could and then flew away. The waters kept rising, and finally it was too late; the man drowned. Upon entering heaven's gates, he asked Saint Peter, "Why didn't the Lord save me?" Saint Peter looked at the man standing before him soaking wet and said, "If you'll wait a moment, I'll go find out." Saint Peter returned with a puzzled look on his face and said, "Our records indicate that God tried saving you three different times—once by ground, once by boat, and

once by air—and each time you refused. Is that
right?" There was nothing heaven's newest resident
could say other than, "May I please have a towel?"

This is a perfect example of how we may get stuck in decision making by believing that God will make the decision
for us. Believing that the essence of faithfulness is surrendering one's will to God's will—"Thy will be done"—it is
easy to see how many persons make decisions by waiting to
see what God wants. But what do we do when it seems that
God has placed us on hold and is not going to return to the
call anytime soon? Moreover, isn't it possible to use the
"waiting on God" rationale as an excuse to avoid making
tough decisions? Are there alternative ways of interpreting
faithfulness that allow us to assume more active and creative
responsibility for the choices we make?

What if genuine faithfulness is less a matter of waiting
on God and more a matter of working or playing with God?
What if God's will is that we will more of our life's destiny,
and not just that, but that we do so
with lavish intent and sensa-
tional joy? Imagine that!

> What
> do we do when
> it seems that God
> has placed us on hold
> and is not going to
> return to the call
> anytime soon?

Note that at the end
of each remaining chap-
ter of this book, you will
find a few exercises to
help you practice and
explore some of the ideas
discussed. Feel free to modify

the directions in ways that best fit you. It is not necessary that you perform each exercise before reading the next chapter. It may be that you'll want to read the book in its entirety and then go back later to select the exercises you wish to complete. However you choose to proceed, you might want to use a journal to record your responses and to facilitate greater freedom of expression. And don't limit your discovery to the points identified on the page. Follow your own lead. Hopefully, that will include creating your own exercises. Above all, relax and have faithful fun! (By the way, if you create an exercise that's especially helpful to you, I would love to know about it. Please e-mail it to me at kjones58@aol.com.)

EXERCISES

1. In a dream you are somewhat startled to hear God say, "Thank you for being so considerate of my will. But you know, more than anything else, my will is for you to do what you really desire doing." Awakening with God's words fresh in your mind, you go to a table and begin writing freely on a sheet of paper, "What I'd really enjoy doing is . . ."

2. Purchase several different versions of a song. The song really doesn't matter. Listen to each version, noting similarities and differences. Once you are done, savor the value of different renditions.

    Now bring this heightened appreciation for different offerings into your reflection about vocation. Allow yourself to playfully consider many different options. Entertain the

notion that there may be numerous vocational opportunities for you of comparable challenge and meaning. Give
yourself permission to choose one or two to focus on
presently.

   (Consider listening and discussing the music with a
friend. Multiple interpretations can make this exercise
even more meaningful.)

3. Claim your strength as a creatively decisive person by
   recalling times you worked yourself out of a "stuck situation." Perhaps it was a traffic jam or a crisis situation that
   demanded urgent ingenuity. Inspired by such instances,
   reflect on your current vocational impasse. Use the memory of your proven strength to move forward.

4. Imagine that all your financial needs are completely satisfied forever. What will you do for work simply for joy's
   sake?

3

the
divine
adventure

F inding one's purpose has become the mission of our time in the United States. The search has several catalysts. First, amid plenty, many Americans have come to realize that more merchandise does not necessarily lead to more meaning. Thousands have felt the gnawing discomfort of having everything and nothing at the same time—everything on the outside and nothing on the inside. This spiritual influenza amid material "affluenza" has prompted many people to search for a deeper meaning, in general, and a vocational life that matters in more deeply satisfying ways, in particular.

Another motivation to the search for purpose has been the impact of numbing tragedies on our shores. The terrorist bombings of September 11, 2001, and the unspeakable devastation of Hurricane Katrina on the Gulf Coast and in my native New Orleans in 2005 are two gigantic reminders that life can be blown or washed away in seconds. In between such unforgettable disasters, round-the-clock news networks and Internet connections keep us abreast of the awesome dynamism and soft fragility of life. In such an environment, many people have been inspired to consider life's realities and potentialities, particularly purpose.

Discovering one's purpose has risen in importance also as a result of the changing employment terrain in our nation. In all but a few jobs, employees no longer have the luxury of job security. Not only does the concept sound archaic; it is archaic. Employees are told to expect and plan for several career transitions during their lifetimes. In the face of multiple vocational decisions at various stages in life, questions of purpose such as "What am I here for?" and "What is God calling me to do?" help us navigate the map of decision making. They help us sift through various opportunities or discern and identify options within ourselves.

Redefining Purpose

Some words that probably come to mind when you hear the word purpose are direction, meaning, objective, and goal. The dictionary definition of purpose is "a thing to be done; an object to be attained, an intention, an aim." In his Dictionary of Word Origins, John Ayto offers that purpose derives from the Latin proponere, which means "put forward, declare." There is a sense of purpose coming from within us as opposed to something that we ascertain apart from us.

Defining purpose as essentially something inside of you helps demystify the whole purpose discernment process by establishing the location of its inspiration. The inspiration for purpose does not come from others. We are often confused as to what we are to do in life because of the many different cues we receive from family and friends. But their good intentions cannot ensure clarity and precision when it comes to our personal ambitions. Besides, often others are communicating what they deeply want for us or what they deeply wanted for themselves but for whatever reasons were never able to realize. That may or may not be what we want for ourselves. Other people can be helpful conversational partners, but they are ill suited to inspire an unqualified and unquestioned sense of purpose in your life. No one knows you like you know you.

The best inspiration for purpose is not events either. Often we are guided to our life's work and actions by circumstances and situations. For example, a child may aspire to becomes a physician based on an experience with a doctor who cared for or healed a loved one. Events may present possibilities, but alone they are insufficient. Desires that derive from a person's essence and evolving sense of self must accompany events. Otherwise, without the sustained approval of the heart, the event that inspired a vocational choice may not be enough to sustain that choice.

One major thing I am asking you to do in this book is to revisit your understanding of purpose and, even more

Without the sustained approval of the heart, the event that inspired a vocational choice may not be enough to sustain that choice.

specifically, your understanding of how your purpose is derived. When I challenged my friend to build her own bridges, I was asking her to go head to head with her stuckness, to take it on, and more deliberately conceptualize and intentionally live her longings. If we are to engage such inner construction work successfully, we must be willing to do one important thing: believe something new. The striking fundamental new belief that moved me from being stuck to realizing my dreams and the basic premise of this book is this:

Purpose is not something we passively receive from God;
purpose is something we actively create with God.

Take some time to think about that statement. Repeat it several times, each time placing the emphasis on different words. Roll the statement around in your head; observe and listen as it bumps up against thoughts you presently hold. What new thoughts does the statement evoke inside you? Does the statement trouble you in any way? Why?

For me, this statement challenges the traditional Christian belief, more recently popularized in the book *The Purpose-Driven Life* by Rick Warren, that discerning our life's purpose is a matter of praying and waiting for God to show us what to do. My view of purpose calls into question the notion that vocational discernment is primarily a matter of receiving prewritten vocational scripts from God. I am convinced that this prevailing belief has had an unintended numbing effect, preventing many of us from perceiving and practicing God's greatest gift: *creative freedom.*

While linking purpose to "God's plan" liberates some people, it leaves others walking around in a deeper vocational fog. The fog may consist of lack of clarity about God's plan or a lack of confidence in such a plan once it is made clear. The fog may also be created by a sense of personal incompetence when it comes to deciphering God's will. The source of powerlessness may be guilt or shame carried by persons who feel they have failed God in the past. The fog of faithlessness may descend from anger persons may have toward God for allowing something to happen they feel should not have happened. Following God's plan presumes that the follower is on speaking terms with God. Often such is not the case. There can be no connecting with God's plan if one is disconnected—even temporarily—from God.

For these reasons and more, many God-fearing people remain dumbfounded when it comes to knowing what they really want to do in life. A middle-aged woman facing a possible career change

> There can be no connecting with God's plan if one is disconnected—even temporarily—from God.

once told me, "It's like living with film over my eyes." Why would a loving God want vocational discernment to be such an elusive and painful enterprise? Why won't God tell you plainly what you are supposed to be doing? Why this holy hide-and-seek?

The answer is in daring to reimagine or redefine the realities we commonly refer to as *purpose, call,* and *vocation.* What if purpose is not something we receive from God but something we create together with God? What if purpose is not something we discover but something we help design? What if, more than anything else, God wants you to experience the joy of searching out and choosing your own purpose in life among a vast assortment of opportunities? What if there isn't a detailed plan for your life but an open outline and an invitation from God to you to creatively and deliberately fill in the spaces? What if God's ultimate dream for your life is that you live and play your best dreams?

> What if purpose is not something we receive from God but something we create together with God?

These questions open us to what I believe is God's fondest desire for us all: assuming free and creative responsibility for imagining and living our best life. I believe that God's primary purpose is that we live free and empowered. Within this marvelous and mysterious expanse, God invites and inspires but never imposes. Indeed, I believe that to prayerfully wait and plead for such an imposition is to unknowingly grieve God.

If God wanted to live your life for you, God would not have created you in the first place. God does not need us helpless in order to be God. We learn such helplessness, sometimes from our theology, and impose it on ourselves. We are challenged to unlearn helplessness and replace it with a soaring sense of sacred empowerment. How ready are you to pick up your freedom and power? How willing are you to accept God's invitation to you, to imagine and create an awesome life? How much are you able to trust that what God wants is for you to want, to earnestly desire and design your own divine purpose, in sacrifice and delight, for the healing of our world?

The Snowfall

What's wrong with believing that discerning our life's purpose is a matter of waiting for God to show us what to do? What's wrong with thinking that deciding what we want to do in life is a matter of finding or receiving prewritten vocational scripts from God? As I write this, it is snowing outside. I have been watching the snowfall's progression from the first faint mist to the fluffy flakes currently filling my kitchen window. If you asked me how many flakes have fallen from the time I first started watching to now, I would say, "Millions." That's just in my backyard. Extend the range just a little and I imagine an unfathomable number of flakes have fallen. Now, I want you to use your imagination. Imagine us, you and I, warmly dressed, walking out into the snowfall together. As you behold the snowflakes, the ones crowded at your feet and the ones swooping down from the sky, imagine that each flake represents an opportunity, a dream, or a life purpose. Suddenly, we hear God's voice say these words: "These are all your possibilities, but I have selected only one for you. Find the one that I have chosen, and live my selection to the best of your ability." With a universe as abundant and vast as ours, why would we think that when it comes to purpose, God would have only one or two things for us to do in life that we must painstakingly discern among all that appears before us? It would be tantamount to God's asking us to select one right snowflake out of a zillion. The whole ordeal would leave us more frustrated than faithful, more paralyzed than empowered.

Imagine God saying something very different to us: "Isn't it wonderful. Each flake represents a purpose, many of which you will love, blessing your life and all life. Go ahead, consider as many dream-flakes as you like. Live fully and freely the ones that give you the most joy and satisfaction. Don't be afraid. Whatever choices you make, know this: I will be with you. Enjoy playing in the snow."

Living Your Purpose with Deliberate Intention and Grand Delight

I have thought long and hard about purpose since my experience on the Hudson River. Many other personal vocational transitions have been discerned and negotiated since then. After reviewing my own journey and countless words of wisdom from mentors, both literary and personal, five thought-actions have emerged as the most important for actively creating your divine purpose. Note that the steps are not sequential; the understanding and exercises associated with each step intersect and may be experienced in various ways over time. For example, the full truth of step one may not be deeply realized until some of the other steps have been taken. Therefore, the following steps are "notes" that may be played in varying order.

> Step One: *Believe that God is your divine partner, not your domineering parent.*
> Step Two: *Believe that vocation is an open possibility, not a closed proposition.*
> Step Three: *Accept that you are not just creature but creator as well.*
> Step Four: *Dream your way to purpose.*
> Step Five: *Joyfully play your dreams.*

In the following chapters, I will discuss each step in detail and provide practical suggestions to help you take each step in your own way. I will also share more of my experiences, as well as others' experiences and words, including biblical testimony. As you journey, you will be introduced to ideas that I hope will bless you as much as they have blessed me. For example, you will learn the grace of "creating from wholeness and not for wholeness." You will discover the importance of "nonanxious dreaming," having visions of accomplishment that are not motivated by fear or the pressing expectations of others. And you will be invited to recover your "play disposition," your innate capacity to express love and lightness of heart in your pursuits. My grandest hope is that when you have finished reading this book, you will be well on your way toward realizing an amazing new life of exhilarating meaning and purpose.

I believe that there is no holier power on earth than the divine energy to deliberately create our lives with God. I challenge you to believe that you have the power and permission from God to make your own vocational choices and build, with God's help and others', your own bridges to a better life. Building your own bridges to what you want to do in life is about continuously broadening your vision of your capacity, responsibly growing your gifts, and tenaciously trusting your dreams.

Getting unstuck and deliberately creating our purpose is infinitely more delightful as we become less and less afraid of having faithful fun and allow ourselves to experience life, purpose and all, as holy play. One early church theologian, Irenaeus, put it enticingly well: "The glory of God is a person fully alive."

I am asking you to trust this new, more open possibility about purpose and to follow your new trust. With God's complete blessing in head and heart, dare to imagine and deliberately create the life of your boldest dreams.

EXERCISES

1. Identify two or three issues about which you have changed your mind. What made you change your thinking?
2. Identify some instances in which changing your beliefs caused you to change your behavior.
3. Overall, how important is *change* to your experience of faith and spirituality?
4. How might changing your understanding of purpose free you to entertain new vocational aspirations and possibilities?

4

our great beloved partner

magine opening your mailbox or e-mail and finding the following message:

> Dear Child:
>
> Although you are an adult, from this day forward I want you to do everything I tell you to do. I will make all of your decisions for you. I will solve your problems. I will tell you what to do and when to do it and how. Your job is to do as I say and trust that living this way is in your best interest.
>
> With deepest love, *God*

Convinced that it was not a hoax, perhaps most of us would be initially numb and then bowled over from having heard from our divine parent in this way. Maybe days and even weeks and months would pass by with our walking on clouds: "God wrote me a letter saying all I have to do is follow instructions! Life is easy!"

How long do you imagine your new joy would last? I know when the thrill would leave me: the second I realized that God had in fact taken from me what had been originally lavishly bestowed on me—human freedom.

Although this letter is special because it is in God's handwriting, the message is, I contend, anything but holy. Take a second look at the letter. Read it again slowly, aloud. If you are honest with yourself, you can almost feel the energy of life oozing out of you.

A friend once told me of an experience she had in her early days as a police officer. When she arrived at one scene and observed a man who was unconscious, she immediately began administering CPR. Soon after, the emergency medical technicians arrived, examined the man, and pronounced him dead. My friend assumed that the man had died while she was administering CPR. She was shocked to learn that the man had been dead for some time. Later reflecting on her experience, she confessed that all the while she was breathing into the man's body, it was as if she was blowing into an empty room. She concluded, "His spirit had already left; there was nothing inside."

Though the imaginary letter from God appears to offer something akin to life; it in fact does nothing of the sort. It is a letter that effectively kills off human freedom and initiative. With this letter, the divine parent essentially usurps the child's right to a free and creative life.

The Letter as Law

This imaginary letter symbolizes the way much of popular Christian thinking views God and vocational discernment. God is pictured as a divine parent who has a set script for our lives. Our job is to discover and pledge allegiance to the script and then spend a lifetime decoding it and living up to it—or else. If the consequences of our own failure don't do us in, it doesn't matter; God will get us later in the afterlife.

Such an understanding results in living bondage. Eliminate human freedom, and life becomes a dreary shade of gray. Belief in a domineering God-parent unintentionally diminishes some of God's greatest gifts to humankind, including imagination, creativity, and daring. It blinds us to the possibility that what God desires most of all is for us to take responsibility for creating our own lives.

As I am writing this, the morning sun is shining mightily in my home office window. Its rays are indicative of brilliantly bright and liberating what-ifs: What if the goal of life is not to live according to a preset script but to write your own script and live it out freely and playfully in the presence of a delightfully expectant and supportive God? What if God's purpose for you is to discover and explore passion after passion, in service to others and to the glory of God? Now, these are laws not just to live by but to dance by!

What's the Appeal of the Domineering God?

Although I am presuming that the freedom-offering God is better than the domineering deity, you may not agree. That kind of parental God is the one we have come to love and need. But think about it. Why is that so?

First, belief in this understanding of God may be because we are holding fast to what we think is all we have. Perceiving God as ordering the course of peoples and nations is a deeply entrenched belief, instilled from an early age. Choosing to believe something different about God may be considered a breach of faith.

Second, a domineering God relieves us of the frustration and tension associated with decision making. As you saw in Chapter Two, on being stuck, deciding our course in life is often a grueling affair, complicated by manifold options and by both supportive and nonsupportive opinions. We compound our dilemma by believing that there is one absolute best choice that offers benefits beyond all other options. Sorting out these options may weigh us down to the point of indecision. Belief that God can and will show and tell us what to do becomes a comforting and viable option. It takes the

A domineering God relieves us of the frustration and tension associated with decision making.

painful risk out of making choices. Of course, the reality is that we often develop another source of pain, the agony of seemingly not being able to hear God's voice and thus being unable to determine God's will.

Third, the domineering God seems to be supported by the book many hold to be the supreme authority in all matters, the Holy Bible. In the Bible, God is seen as delivering divine edicts (the Ten Commandments), calling individuals to special missions (Moses and the prophets), and determining when and how God's people are to be freed from bondage (the Exodus). This divine rulership is laced with the knowledge that God loves and cares. Indeed, one of the most deeply cherished and repeated texts of all is David's Twenty-Third Psalm, a litany of divine loving guidance in which the divine "makes us lie down in green pastures and leads us beside still waters." If God is domineering, it is for our sake, and it must therefore be accepted, endured, and appreciated.

The ultimate biblical mandate that many people repeat, if mindlessly, daily is "Thy will be done on earth as it is in heaven." For all the talk of human freedom, in the Bible, it is perceived as being subject to God's ultimate overriding will. Devout believers should be less interested in exploring the parameters of human freedom than in decoding the mysterious but ultimately perfect and supreme will of God. Unable to grasp the scope of God's will, we usually end up perceiving it narrowly. But that's not our biggest fault. Our biggest error comes in pressuring others to conform to our understanding of God's perfect will. We end up

getting tied up in the long string of arguments and con-
tentions regarding God's will for public life and personal
decisions. In the middle of it all, God's holy question to
each of us lingers unnoticed: What is it that *you* really want?

The domineering God is also a check against chaos in
our world and in our lives. As long as God is in charge, we
can count on all things happening ultimately as they
should. I remember hearing in the church of my youth the
religious adage spoken in the face
of unexplainable woe: "God is
still on the throne." Evil
may get by, but it will not
get away.

The problem here
is that it keeps us from
realizing the sacredness of
tension and chaos. All tension is not destructive; all
chaos is not unproductive. There
is a creative tension without which there can be no growth
and development. In his marvelous book *Callings: Finding and Following an Authentic Life*, Gregg Levoy finds a model
for the fruitfulness of chaos in nature. He likens contrary
forces inside of us to ecotones: "Either way, the oppos-
ing forces occupy a space that is like an ecotone, a transition
zone between two ecological communities like forest and
grassland or river and desert. They compete, yes; the word
ecotone means a house divided, a system in tension. But they
also exchange, swapping juices, information, and resources.

> Our biggest error comes in pressuring others to conform to *our* understanding of God's perfect will.

Ecotones have tremendous biological diversity and resilience."

It is possible to believe that God may work within chaos to help us identify and unearth all-too-familiar truths that have outlived their usefulness in our lives. Feeling that something is wrong and experiencing the accompanying tension may in fact be birth pangs, gracious signs of new life.

We will return to this matter throughout the remainder of the book. We can learn to hear tension as a necessary part of the ongoing music of life, a part not to be shunned but to be sung through in sacrifice and sometimes in surprising delight.

Discomforting tension may be the most underappreciated reality in the universe. Looking back on my own twists and turns, I can now see that some of my most thrilling and fulfilling adventures were ushered in by a period of almost overwhelming malaise. It is a terrible thing to be completely comfortable for too long.

Finally, the domineering God appeals to us because it comes encased in the seeming undisputed argument that God knows best. God's wisdom transcends our rational and unconscious sources of inspiration. Why not appeal to God for advice and decisions?

For the faithful, it foolish not to do so. The problem with this view is that it keeps adherents dependent, denied the right to and grow through making their own decisions. Theologically speaking, what makes matters worse is that freedom may be the gift God wants most for us to experience. By refusing it, we reject what God wants to give us most of all.

In my imagination, I see a push and pull going on. God keeps trying to gently place freedom, with the accompanying intention and purpose, into our hands, and we keep giving it back, saying, "No, thanks." We perceive this refuting of freedom as doing God a favor, as honoring God: "Thy will be done." Such a posture needs to be redeemed by an expanded understanding of God, one that allows us to perceive God's will as being open and inclusive of human desire and decision. God doesn't want to tell us what to do or make us do anything. More than ordaining and demanding, God dialogues with and inspires us. The choice is always, always ours, to make and live through, with God at our side.

> Freedom may be the gift God wants most for us to experience. By refusing it, we reject what God wants to give us most of all.

Losing and loosing an image of God as a domineering parent is energizing and freeing. Energy spent on decoding God's will can now be used to freely explore all the God-inspired desires of our hearts. Fear that we will mistake something else for God's will dissolves in the face of God's lavish grace, which envisions our being able to bless the world in manifold ways and callings. Tension and frustrations are not immediately perceived as signs of estrangement from God but rather as indicators of genuine stretching and adventuring into dynamically threatening and enlivening new territories.

The other huge benefit to changing our view of God as a domineering parent is that we open ourselves to engaging a God who yearns for dialogue—to inspire us and, wonder of wonders, perhaps to even be inspired.

A God of Dialogue

A man tending his sheep suddenly spots something worth seeing, a bush holding its form while on fire. Moments after positioning himself to get a better view, the man hears a voice that begins a conversation between a mysterious presence and Moses. His life—and the lives of thousands of people—will be transformed.

We can read the call of Moses as God mandating him with a mission that he had to accept. It was in the divine cards. After all, Moses had been rescued from sure death as an infant by Pharoah's daughter and protected from all harm as a resident in Pharoah's home. It was his undeniable destiny to liberate his people.

But before we accept this interpretation, let's think about the whole notion of "call." Calls are not orders; they are appeals that ask for a response. A call is an opportunity, not a mandate, an invitation that we are free to explore and either accept or reject with the assurance that rejection does not separate us from the will or love of God. God's will and love are much too big for that.

With regard to Moses' call, it is noteworthy that God does not speak to Moses right away, when he catches sight of the flaming shrubbery with his peripheral vision. Not until Moses "turns aside to see" does God call out to him from the bush. From the beginning, the call assumes a dialogue, a conversation. What would have happened had Moses not turned to look at the burning bush? We don't know. But we can see that the call hinges not on God's forcefulness but on Moses' curiosity and continuing interest. God supplies the invitation; Moses has to supply the acceptance.

> Calls are not orders; they are appeals that ask for a response.

In fact, the dance between divine invitation and human acceptance continues for two entire chapters. God and Moses go back and forth on the specifics of the liberation plan. It is a fascinating exchange in which Moses wins a major concession: While it may have been God's original intent for Moses to confront Pharaoh alone, at Moses' urging, God reconsiders, and Moses' brother, Aaron, is envisioned as a liberator along with Moses. A spirit of collaboration is evident in the exchange between God and Moses from beginning to end. Even though God's intentional inspiration is the primary catalyst in the narrative, the story turns one way or the other on Moses' response. God's purpose is actualized through divine call and human response.

Consider another legendary calling, God's call to Mary to bear Jesus. An initial reading of this magnificent calling in Luke's gospel suggests that it runs counter to the argument I am making against a domineering deity. The angel Gabriel's announcement is filled with will's: "You will conceive in your womb." "You will name him Jesus." "The Holy Spirit will come upon you." Can divinity be any more overbearing than that? It appears as if the matter and method of Jesus' entry into the world is a "done deal." Mary is simply expected to do as she is told, case closed. But keep reading and listening. The angel, God's representative, does not have the final word. He says what he has to say and then waits. That's right; he waits with angelic mouth shut. His mission, it turns out, is not merely to tender something but to receive something. That something is Mary's consent.

One wonders about the space, the pause between Gabriel's articulation of divine vision and Mary's expression of human volition. Are we to surmise that Mary really agreed to such a wild, if divine, destiny without pause, wonder, and worry? Could she possibly have wiped her eyes and blinked several times, thinking that the angel was a figment of her imagination

"You will conceive in your womb." "You will name him Jesus." "The Holy Spirit will come upon you." Can divinity be any more overbearing than that?

who would vanish as suddenly as he had appeared? Once she was convinced that she really was in the presence of an angel, could she have thought, "Thanks, but no thanks"? Might she have considered inviting the angel to return a week or two later after she had had time to think about it? Or did she secretly plan to go into hiding? We don't know, but we do know that God needed Mary's assent. We diminish the power of the gospel when we seek to sanitize it of all human expression and possibility.

The meeting between Mary and Gabriel is not a monologue; it is a dialogue. And the dialogue is not over until Mary offers her consent, which she renders as follows: "Here am I, the servant of the Lord; let it be with me according to your word." Only after hearing this does Gabriel depart from her presence. The meaning may be startling to some but nevertheless undeniably true: God calls Mary but leaves Mary free to offer her genuine and honest response. She is not forced to be the mother of the Savior; she is *invited* to be. Accordingly, God does not impose vocation on us; God inspires vocation.

Even for Jesus, the dialogical nature of his divine calling and mission is evident throughout his life. Though, I believe, confronted with an awesome sense of daring destiny from the beginning, God's call never denies Jesus the opportunity of free response. In spite of God's promptings and urgings, Jesus is always free to design his own destiny. In Luke 4, the temptation of Jesus, he considers other ethical alternatives and chooses the way he believes to be God-inspired. In that same chapter, he speaks of being "anointed to bring good news to the poor, proclaim release to the captives, recovery of sight to the blind, to let the oppressed go free, and to proclaim the year of the Lord's favor." But it is Jesus who has to choose to keep listening to the vision and keep leaning into it amid grown tensions and hostilities—those inside of him and those mounting in the hearts of friends and enemies around him.

Jesus' habitual treks into the mountains or to the sea for solitude can be seen as sessions to allow divine urgings to bubble up inside of him. His momentous final session in the garden on the night he was betrayed highlights the radically back-and-forth nature of his relationship with the deity, a God he comfortably referred to with the strongly personal Abba ("Father"). In the Garden of Gethsemane, we clearly hear that his destiny is in fact his choosing what he perceives to be God's will: "Father, if you are willing, remove this cup from me; yet not my will but yours be done." God never forces Jesus to do anything; Jesus lives a life of free choice in loving, if at times trying, response to divine inspiration.

> God never forces Jesus to do anything; Jesus lives a life of free choice in loving, if at times trying, response to divine inspiration.

Though God is portrayed as having forthright intention, God's vision is not forced on Moses, Mary, or Jesus. God honors the precious gift of human freedom.

Reenvisioning God

How do you envision God? Following are some common impressions of God I have gleaned from my religious experience and more than two decades of pastoral ministry and seminary teaching. First read them, adding more of your own if you desire. Next, go back and select the two or three designations of God that best express the way you experience divinity in your life. You may want to identify the way you have experienced God in the past and the single-word definition that most appeals to you now.

Guide	Creator	Friend	Provider
Father	Supporter	Source	Mystery
Mother	Parent	Judge	_____
Ruler	Companion	Spirit	_____

As you view the list and your own selections, consider this question: Does your designation of God allow for your own dynamic creative expression? I believe there are ways of viewing God that have the unintended (and I would argue ungodly) effect of diminishing human creativity and ingenuity. For example, a view of God as judge may go a long way toward limiting freedom of expression. We hush ourselves for fear that what we present may not be pleasing to God. Even an innocent and respectful estimation of God as the source can do unwitting damage. Is God the only source of inventiveness and creativity? Or has God placed a considerable amount of divine genius in every human heart? If the latter is true, it is not enough to look elsewhere for the source, one must learn to honor and trust the source within, one's own inner spring of wisdom and insight. This is the God-endowed human creative power that Sue Monk Kidd writes about in her enchanting novel *The Secret Life of Bees*. The spiritual mentor August explains to fourteen-year-old Lilly that extraordinary power is not to be deposited exclusively in the objects and symbols of religious affection. Genuine, passionate dynamism is within:

> "Our Lady is not some magical being out there
> somewhere, like a fairy godmother. She's not the
> statue in the parlor. She's something *inside* of you. Do
> you understand what I am telling you?
>
> "You have to find the mother inside yourself. We
> all do. Even if we already have a mother, we still
> have to find this part of ourselves inside."

Although Jesus constantly referred to God as Father, an intimate Holy Other, with no less conviction did he freely and regularly speak about the kingdom of God being *inside* of us. His understanding of God embellished humanity; it did not diminish what it means to be human.

Here's the question: Does your understanding of God release you or hold you back? If you find your understanding of God restricting rather than unleashing your human fire of desire and choice, you would do well to expand your understanding of God. Your more passionate and fulfilling life depends on it.

Taking Out the Garbage

I have just returned to my writing from a Monday morning ritual: taking out the garbage. Along with the usual trash, my collection included an old carpet. The ugly orange piece of rug was, twenty years ago, the glory under someone's feet. But through wear and tear, its original brilliance had dissipated with the years. It occurred to me that the carpet was in a way like our first views of God. They were undoubtedly striking and brought great comfort, a sense of cosmic protection. Yet seeing God exclusively as omnipotent, protective parent, judge, and ruler has a significant drawback: dependency. If we are not careful, we will never come into our own glory, our own strength, if we remain fixated on a Divine Power we believe is intent on wielding, not sharing, the creative energy of life. So we need to change the carpet of our thoughts and beliefs about God.

We also need to toss out another kind of thinking about God: theological "adult" ponderings about God that prevent "childlike" whimsical, playful interpretations of God. We don't need to think more "adult thoughts"—closed and rigid—about God. It seems to me that most adult thinking about God ends up having divinity looking and behaving too similarly to the adult. And often this God is pitted against the understandings and ways of others in a bid for philosophical and theological supremacy. No! We don't need any more "adult thinking" about God.

Enter more childlike thoughts about God. Enter a God who prances, dances, smiles, and laughs. Enter a God who's greatest use of power is gifting it. Enter a God who believes that rainbows are for walking, not simply viewing. Enter a God who lives in an ocean of imagination and wonder and loves it no end when children and adults jump in for the faithful fun of it! But most of all, enter a God who walks, speaks, and sings new songs of inspiration and fulfill-ment—and sings them with us.

Seeing God, Yourself, and Vocation in New Ways

Seeing God in freer, more fanciful ways inspires free and fanciful vocational expression. Vocational discernment is no longer a matter of being weighted down by what God demands but rather of being liberated to unleash our voca-tions in adventurous freedom. This God is our loving, play-ful partner in daringly and joyfully creating and re-creating life, moment by moment.

I conclude my first book, *Rest in the Storm: Self-Care Strategies for Clergy and Other Caregivers*, with a sermon, "Let There Be Laughter." The sermon climaxes as follows:

> Dario Fo, one of Italy's great playwrights and
> clowns, won the 1997 Nobel Prize for literature.

When he was first informed of this, he thought it
was a big joke. Assured and reassured that it was
not, Fo exclaimed, "God is a clown!"

God is a clown. We do not find these exact words
in Scriptures, but we do find these words:

A happy heat makes the face cheerful. (Proverbs
    15:13)
The cheerful heart has a continual feast. (Proverbs
    15:15)
Everlasting joy will crown their heads. Gladness and
    joy will overtake them, and sorrow and sighing
    will flee. (Isaiah 35:10)
For I will turn their mourning into gladness; I will
    give them comfort and joy instead of sorrow.
    (Jeremiah 31:13)
I bring you good news of great joy that will be for
    all the people. (Luke 2:10)
Blessed are you who weep now, for you will laugh.
    (Luke 6:21)
Ask and you will receive, and your joy will be
    complete. (John 16:24)
[God] will wipe every tear from their eyes.
    (Revelation 21:4)

You may find this clown-talk about a God who dances
and sings disrespectful. (I was once criticized by a well-
meaning deacon for being "too playful" in the pulpit. Many
years later, I now regard it as one of the best compliments I
have ever received.) Perhaps you feel that I am being too
playful about the sacred. What good are understandings of
God that snuff the joy out of life? Are stuffy understandings

of God the stuff of sacred spirited living? How fancifully ought we allow ourselves to think about God as presented in the Christian faith? Well, let's see. We read of a God who turns seas into highways, whales into transport vessels, and lions' dens into prayer rooms. In the New Testament, we are presented with God in a man named Jesus who turns water into wine, walks on water, heals without medicine, and stares down death more than once for others, as well as for himself. The biblical record cries out for a God, shall we say, a bit less respectful and restrained than our rituals and practices infer and seem to prefer.

If you are able to see God in dynamic new ways, you will be able to see yourself and your potential in dynamic new ways. This has been true in my experience. Opening up my understanding of God and God's will has given me permission to ponder and pursue various vocational impulses. Take writing, for instance. If you would have suggested to me ten years ago that I would be experiencing great fulfillment as a writer, I would have looked at you as if you were from another planet. I enjoyed preaching and being a church pastor too much to be distracted by writing. But wider notions of God consciously and unconsciously broadened me and my perception of my capacities and possibilities. Lighter, more spacious understandings of God coaxed me toward a living openness that inspired greater visions of who I was and who I could become. Self-imposed restriction gave way to Spirit-inspired expanse.

Allow me to share two alternative images of God that have stretched me and my experience with vocation. The first is God as a jazz musician. The image is inspired by the soul-stunning remarks attributed to jazz musicians regarding creativity and imagination. Edward Kennedy "Duke" Ellington always said that his favorite composition was "his next one." Mary Lou Williams spoke of being so in tune with musicians she was playing with that she could "hear the note he was going to play next." Miles Davis

If you are able to see God in dynamic new ways, you will be able to see yourself and your potential in dynamic new ways

encouraged musicians to "go beyond themselves, to the new place, and the next place he is going, and even beyond that." Jimmy Scott explains that he sings very slowly because he believes in the beat, and "the beat sets you free." When Ella Fitzgerald sings "Reach for Tomorrow," I am moved to tears and fresh new energy for life and ministry. Such heartfelt expressions of artistic vitality enflame me. These and similar sentiments from the saints of jazz ooze with sanctified zest that can have no other source than the ultimate creative reality, God. Perceiving God in such a way predisposes me to experience life and vocational calling in more creative and dynamic ways.

My other understanding of God, and perhaps the one I picture the most and the most easily, is God as an expansive ocean of unconditional love. This image came one day years ago when I was fathoming God's ability to bear the brokenness and grief of all history. As I begin to imagine God's tears, those tears formed a body of water that somehow, I comfortingly perceived, was sufficient enough to "bear and transform it all."

Since then, this body of water has become a source of daily strength for me as I imagine myself swimming, floating, and playing in it. The waters energize and sooth my soul. They fill me with joy and gratitude for life and relationships. They inspire creative insights and connections. It is one thing to sing, "Jesus loves me, this I know, for the Bible tells me so." It is another thing entirely to *feel* God's love each day, sometimes several times a day.

What does seeing God as a jazz musician and as a body of water have to do with purpose? By envisioning God in such creative and open ways rather than as a God who judges and rules, we develop a creatively open disposition. We develop an inclination toward life that is broader, wider, and grander. We develop an unconscious distaste and suspicion for narrowness of any sort, including the kind that afflicts much of our thinking about life's vocation and purpose.

Begin today envisioning God in new and imaginative ways. Breaking open your understandings of God will have the effect of breaking open your understanding of life and your life's dreams and purposes. Become more creatively free in interpreting divinity frees you to think about life's possibilities in new and exciting ways. The hallelujah ripple effect of thinking about God expansively is that you can begin to conceptualize your aspirations in ever-expanding new ways.

Heavy, domineering notions of God cause us to have burdensome perceptions of life. The goal is to develop new notions of God that galvanize you and set you free. The possible images of God are endless, as expansive as God's universe that we are presently being told by scientists is everexpanding. The goal, I believe, is to create images of God that are lighter and wider than the images we are accustomed to, images that enlarge rather than diminish our divinely endowed human spirits.

Alternative images of God inspire broader and more creative interpretations of such things as life's purpose, something we tend to interpret restrictively and narrowly. Expand your understanding of God and you expand your understanding of divine purpose. Fill your understanding of God with more joyful, playful, and freeing perspectives, and realizing purpose becomes a more joyful, playful, and freeing enterprise.

Easing the restrictions and burdensomeness associated with popular Christian perspectives about discerning purpose begins with nullifying and replacing our limited and heavy-laden ways of perceiving God. Set God free, and life is more easily perceived as a divine freedom practice—even play. When it comes to perceiving purpose, God does not frustrate and hinder us; we do through what we believe about God. Changing your perception about God has the power to unleash powerful new creative energy inside you. Changing your belief about God will light your imagination, causing you to see possibilities and prospects for your life you never imagined before.

EXERCISES

1. Close your eyes, relax your body, and empty your mind of all thoughts. For a moment, try not to think about anything at all. You may find that imagining emptiness (an empty container or a vacant house, for example) useful in helping you to achieve mental stillness. Once you have achieved mental quiet, say the word *God* silently to yourself. Visualize the mental images that the word conjures up. If you are of a mind to, sketch a picture of your images in your journal. After a minute of viewing these images, open your eyes. Write down some of the pictures of God that entered your mind. Reflect on them. Ask yourself, "Do my images of God hold me down or set me free?" Ask yourself about the reasons for your answer.

2. Did you know that writing with your nondominant hand can create greater openness to new perceptions and understandings? First, achieve mental stillness as in Exercise 1. Then, using your nondominant hand, complete the following sentence:

Strangely enough, I can see God as . . .

After you have finished writing, reflect on how your new understandings of God makes you feel. Remain open to your new vision. Be ready to notice, catch, and create more fresh thoughts about God and life. Bring this spirit and mind-set to your current and future thinking about your life's goals and purpose. Record your new perceptions in your journal.

5

the wild thrill of wide-open possibility

When I was younger, if you had asked me what my purpose in life was, I would have told you it was to preach the gospel. Though no one in my immediate family was a minister, I talked about being a preacher as early as seven or eight years old. At ten, after observing a film clip of a mesmerizing man named Martin Luther King Jr., who spoke of having been to the mountaintop on the eve of his death, my purpose was sealed. I *knew* I would become a minister, and Martin Luther King Jr. personified the kind of minister I wanted to be.

I did become a minister and pastor to four different churches. I was fulfilled until, as you read earlier, I experienced vocational rumblings in New Orleans. Suddenly, I found myself flirting with a call to teach, and eventually with what I am doing now, writing. The writing call was an even bigger surprise to me than the compelling desire to teach. However, I can trace its steps even more distinctly than my prior two vocations.

Having been a boy preacher, my focus had always been on the spoken word. So I was as surprised as anyone when I began noticing a growing passion for writing. Looking back, I now realize that the seeds for my writing joy were present even in my boyhood preacher days: I *wrote* all of my sermons. My writing continued through class papers, doctoral examinations and dissertations, and sermons I crafted for publication. But through most of it, I was fixated on the finished product, not the fine process of writing itself.

A series of inspirations ignited my interest in writing for writing's sake. First, Edward Long Jr., an eminent social ethicist at Drew University, wisely and gently informed me one day that being a good speaker and being a good writer were two different things. I learned that tools that make for good sermonizing, such as voice inflection and facial expression, are not at a writer's disposal. Consequently, writers must compensate by using different methods to communicate effectively. If I was going to improve as a writer, I would have to practice—with deliberate and sustained awareness—efficient punctuation, precise word selection, compelling sentence structure, and more.

My second inspiration came through reading Brenda Ueland's classic *If You Want to Write*. In her inspiring and enchanting writing manifesto, Ueland encourages her readers to write "like a child stringing beads in kindergarten—

happy, absorbed, and quietly putting one bead on after another." Linking writing to playfulness created enormous new energy in me for learning more about writing and for writing more.

My third writing inspiration was reading the following words by the beloved spiritual teacher Henri Nouwen: "As we simply sit down in front of a sheet of paper and start to express in words what is in our minds or in our hearts, new ideas emerge, ideas that can surprise us and lead us to inner places we hardly knew were there." These words, combined with a growing appreciation for the musical cosmic wonder commonly referred to as jazz, sensitized me to the creative power of writing. Writing was not just a matter of *recording* ideas but also of *generating* ideas! For three to four hours in the morning, five or six days a week, I write—or play—for delight and discovery.

Reflecting on my vocational journey, only the beginning of which I had previously envisioned, I can see how one decision was crucial above all others: the decision to redefine purpose as something open and evolving as opposed to something closed and settled.

Undoing Predetermined Purpose

In my own life, I have had to come to terms with a belief that I was divinely predestined to be something that was beyond any human altering or choosing. Earlier in my life, when I spoke of discerning vocation, I saw it as diligently

searching for a secret etched in stone. If I could find the
stone and decipher the secret, I will have found my purpose
in life.

Thinking this way, I seemed to have found the stone
early in life. I was comfortable in my preaching aspiration
and even had a thematic Scripture that served as a touch-
stone: "Whom shall I send? And who will go for us? And I
said, 'Here am I, send me'" (Isaiah 6:8). Considering what
happened from the perspective of nearly forty years later, I
can interpret my calling as one of several invitations from
God. I don't believe that it was "preach or else" for me. Such
a view runs counter to the loving free essence of God that
pervades Scripture.

Believing that one's purpose is set in stone can be a
formidable obstacle to entertaining a wide variety of possible vocational considerations. It can keep us from freely
pursuing curiosities and passions, and it can make us resistant to a new passion when one shows up. When we believe
that what we are called to do is final, we may perceive legit-
imate sacred desires as *threats* to godliness as opposed to the
treats from God that they often are.

The truth is that early in my life, I entertained a number of interests and at points thought about doing a
number of things when I grew up, including playing foot-
ball and being a ventriloquist. (I don't know where the latter came from, but it was there.) I was fascinated by all of
my subjects in elementary school, especially history,
English, and physical education. As I went through junior
high and high school, instrumental and vocal music cap-

tured my interest, as well as journalism, drama, and politi-
cal science. Along the way, I had teachers in all of these
fields affirming my gifts and possible contributions.

As it turned out, I remained with the pursuit that had
settled inside me earliest. I pursued a career in ministry.
Helping the decision along was my special-student status at
a small Bible college. After attending school in the day, three
nights a week I sat in classes for three hours at Union Baptist
Theological Seminary in New Orleans. My fate was further
sealed by the fact that I was preaching most Sundays. It
wasn't so much a decision to become what I desired to be
but to continue being who I already was.

Given my own early commitment and zeal for ministry, was my destiny set? Was my purpose predetermined?
Though there may have been a time when I would have said
it was, I now answer with an unqualified and even delighted, "No." In spite of the early inclinations and impulses
toward ministry, it was always my choice to follow that
blessed path or travel another that was no less blessed.

We need to accept complete
freedom as we pursue vocation. Sacrificing freedom,
even to God, nullifies
dynamic creative energy
we need to imagine our
vocational possibility in
its fullness. Sacrificing
freedom especially to God
is tragic. Not feeling free to

> Not feeling free to imagine everything diminishes our capacity to imagine anything.

imagine everything diminishes our capacity to imagine any-thing. This is the source of a great deal of vocational stuck-ness. We limit ourselves as we believe God has limited us. Not wanting to disobey God, when we feel joylessness about a calling we believe to be God-ordained, we choose the lesser evil: being stuck.

Allow yourself to believe that purpose is much more of an open reality, and you open yourself up to tantalizing new possibilities for your life. It is impossible for us to be free beings before God and puppets at the same time.

During my morning meditation time, I often visual-ize emptiness as a way of making space to engage mystery in fresh new ways, without familiar or preferred experi-ences getting in the way. I may use my imagination to envi-sion an empty house with doors and windows flung wide open or a cloudless sky or an empty pitcher overturned with the last drop of its contents falling to the ground. I clear my mind of all thought for a moment so that I can experience God on God's own terms in a fresh new way. While doing this exercise, I am open to new images of emptiness; indeed, some-times I ask for them in my heart. One morning, the image of a book came to the fore. As I remained with the image, I perceived it as having a golden cover, and it

> God has chosen neither to write nor to dictate the script for our lives. That is our calling, our job, our play.

was closed. Suddenly, a gust of wind blew it open. What did I see? Nothing. Absolutely nothing. The pages of this text draped in gold held no words. There was no script. Suddenly, I had a new powerful image of emptiness.

I think of the book as it relates to this discussion. Purpose is a golden open book awaiting the entry of our precious desires and dreams. In respect of sacred freedom, God has chosen neither to write nor to dictate the script for our lives. That is our calling, our job, our play. God is waiting with glorious anticipation for you to pick up the pen of desires and dreams and write what you will write and live what you will live—as fearlessly as you possibly and impossibly can.

The Myth of Singular Divine Purpose

At my own junctures of vocational change, I faced a formidable challenge: the view that the preaching ministry was the only thing that I had been truly called to do. I now refer to this as the "myth of singular divine purpose." In my life, the myth went like this: Certainly I was to preach and preach only. Why else would I feel called to do it so early in life? It was my favorite and most developed skill. Everyone affirmed and encouraged my continuing effectiveness and growth. And maybe, proof perfect, pastors in the African American church don't just leave the preaching and pastoral ministry to do something else. Once a pastor, always a pastor. Where I grew up, preacher-pastors had been known to remain in their churches for thirty or forty years or more.

My own home church, Mount Hermon Baptist Church in New Orleans, had had only four pastors in its more than one hundred year history.

To embrace two other full-time careers (first teaching and then writing), I had to get beyond understanding purpose as a single overriding divine calling, as God's only indisputable desire, that and nothing else. I had to give myself permission to believe that life could include multiple divine callings and that each could be observed fully and delightfully in its own season and at its own time.

The myth of singular divine purpose can trap us in the pit of vocational drudgery. It is possible to feel the joyful calls of other vocations but resist them in the belief that God's vocational will has already been completely established and manifested in our lives, whether we like it or not. This is further reinforced by the belief that we are called to do what we do best. We value established skills over new possibilities. However, exclusively clinging to what we are most skillful at is a sure way to never become skillful at anything else. Helping me face down the myth of divine singular calling was a belief that to this day thrills me to no end: the possibility of multiple expanding vocational passions.

> Exclusively clinging to what we are most skillful at is a sure way to never become skillful at anything else.

Did you read the last sentence carefully? If so, you'll see that I didn't say, "multiple expanding vocational *callings*." I said, "multiple expanding vocational *passions*." A whole new energy is released for our worklife when we (1) believe that what we are called to do is connected to our passions and (2) believe that our passions may change over life and hence our vocations. Purpose is not some supreme endeavor; purpose is the sum total of your passions and endeavors.

To find your purpose, touch your fire, your passions. To live your purpose to the fullest, get used to manifesting the changing colors and directions of multiple flames over the span of your life. Purpose is not a restricted labor imposed by God. Purpose is an unrestricted passion inspired by God. Moreover, purpose is not a single endeavor; purpose is the sum total of our vocational expressions lived in ever-expanding measurements of sacrifice and delight.

Purpose and Passion

I would have eliminated some of my consternation surrounding my vocational shifts if I had granted more weight to what I was feeling inside. For example, when I shifted from pastoral ministry to teaching full time, I began noticing how often I would lose a sense of time while in the midst of a lively classroom discussion. I noted that the intense classroom joy was akin to the fulfilling experiences I'd had in the pastorate.

At first, this joy in a strange land was threatening to me. There was a sense of not wanting this experience to rival my familiar and long-standing commitment to preaching and leading in a local church. Part of me wanted to deny or at least mute my classroom thrill out of a desire to protect my devotion to what I was already doing. After all, God had "called" me to preach and pastor. This was my purpose in life. I presumed that my purpose had been fixed and that anything else that commandeered my desire was not of God and thus a vital threat to my sacred, authentic purpose. But what I have since learned is that God communicates purpose directly through our passions, and there is no limit to how many passions we can have. There is a limit in terms of our being able to live out our passions within the span of our human lives, but there is no limit to the number of things we can love, explore, and manifest as we are inspired to do so by an eternal God. Can you feel, as I did, the freedom, possibility, and even playfulness in such a perspective?

Vocational expression is not isolating a skill and living it through to the point of boredom. Vocational expression is a celebration of successive living passions, a public manifestation of the holy dreams and offerings that that live—and burn—inside us.

If you are confused about what you are called to do, the surest way to achieve clarity and confidence is to identify what excites and ignites you. If you are at a loss when it comes to naming such things, begin with identifying

what you are curious about.
As someone once said,
"Genius is a child chas-
ing a butterfly up a
mountain." You'll know
what a passion is. It is
something you find easy
to talk about. Passion is
something others notice easily, even if you don't at all. It is
what you love, what you are curious about, what preoccu-
pies you. Purpose is not some mysterious entity that God
imposes on us for God's own sake; purpose is the expression of passion. Is it so hard to allow yourself to believe
that God wants you to do what you most readily and easily in your heart want to do?

God communicates purpose directly through our passions, and there is no limit to how many passions we can have.

When it comes to purpose, I think many Christians
and other spiritually motivated people are stuck looking in
the wrong direction: outward. The book of Acts records a
final departure of the risen Jesus. As he ascends, the first
courageous followers fixate on his presence rising higher
and higher above them, to the point at which they can no
longer see him. But they keep looking up. Their gaze is fixed
on the sky above them. Perhaps they would have been there
long into the night and maybe even the next day, still looking up, if it were not for angelic beings who break in and
encourage them to move on. Over the next weeks, they
learn that their spiritual growth will hinge not on looking

outside of themselves but on looking within and feeling a dynamic new Holy Spirit of liberating empowerment.

Looking within is the surest way to increased clarity about most matters, including vocational discernment. The best spiritual teachers and guides are those who don't give us answers from on high but help us initiate our journeys within, where all the answers are. That is why I heed Jesus' admonition for us to notice to the kingdom of God on the inside of each one of us. Many people tend to look up and out for a "word from God" or an event or occurrence, "a sign," or seek wisdom from sainted sages whom we presume know more about us then we know about ourselves. With all due respect to these revered modes of revelations, our wholesome desires and passions are no less sacred than outer words, signs, and pronouncements. For sure, we should attend to outward signs and influences—bushes are still burning—but in the end, such signals must be routed through the soul's seeing and sensing. When all is said and done, our inner passions are the most important guides to vocational opportunities and pursuits.

I can now see that this inner journey was important for my first calling as a preacher-pastor. In fact, I was not pursuing a profession or a role; from the beginning, I was following a fire burning inside of me. I enjoyed Bible stories. I was entranced by the company and guidance and exploits of a Mysterious Other. I enjoyed stringing words together and saying them in such away that inspired and sometimes even excited others. It was not about being a preacher per se; it was about living out what was *outstanding* inside of me.

What's *out* and *standing* inside of you? What wakes you up at night? What do you find yourself thinking about when you should be thinking about something else? Heartfelt passions are God's ways of getting our attention, of "calling us." Don't shun your passions or try to hush them. Pursue your passions. Indeed, give them a standing ovation, as they are your best guides to vocational fulfillment.

The Question That Secretly Binds

Several years ago, a I heard a lecture titled "Killing Us Softly." The presenter spoke of the ways in which American culture is damaged by media advertising that perpetuates sexism against women in our country and throughout the world. The images are often innocent, soft, and seemingly decent. As such, they are received and digested without question. They are never perceived as causing harm. But by not making ourselves aware of the underlying messages in this kind of advertising, argued the professor, we unconsciously accept realities that diminish us. We unknowingly participate in our own destruction, all the while oblivious to the serious damage being done.

Similarly, if not as dramatically, we risk harming ourselves if we don't question the questions we ask. For example, there is a question that is particularly popular in Christian circles. Perhaps the most frequently asked question by Christians seeking spiritual guidance surrounding their purpose is "What is God's will for my life?" The question is

so respectfully righteous, it would appear to be beyond challenge. But challenge it we must if we are to overcome limiting beliefs about God and purpose. At first glance, the question is wholly positive. It presupposes that life is about
something beyond mere existence. It acknowledges "something else," an entity that is beyond us, thus assuring our
connection to something larger than ourselves. The question
promotes living larger. Moreover, the question is a check
against overly self-absorbed existence. Sure, it is my life, but
I am not the only one who has something to say about it.
The question promotes a divine-human relationship.

Nevertheless, the question "What is God's will for my
life?" can diminish us in subtle but lethal ways. This question, in seeking to dislodge information regarding our life's
purpose, can, without evoking the slightest suspicion, hide
our vision of purpose.

The first problem with the question is that it may be
forever unanswerable, depending on how close you feel to
God. To expect a God that you may ordinarily feel distant
from to be forthcoming on a matter as practical and personal as human purpose is to set yourself up for certain disap-
pointment. Your understanding of God mostly as a distant
mysterious other may sabotage your efforts to hear from
God on matters of everyday meaning and importance.

The second problem with the question is that it presupposes that God has already constructed a script for your
life that God expects you to fulfill. This perspective disallows
the real possibility that there are no divine scripts, that God's
will for us is a blank page that we are to complete together

wedded to work that is financially rewarding but little else is tragic. Shackles are shackles, even if they happen to be made of gold.

As you redefine your purpose for yourself, be open to interpreting it less as a singular, familiar, even optimal vocational expression and more as the sum total of a variety of vocational expressions over the span of your life. Theologically speaking, God does not call us to one "best" or "perfect" ambition. God calls us to many experiences, all of which offer grand and glorious opportunities for growth and gift-giving to the world.

The Changing Workplace and Changing Passions

Times and things have changed when it comes to work habits and patterns in the United States. The employee who remained in a position for decades or with the same company out of loyalty, like the organization's reciprocal loyalty, is a relic of the past. Because of downsizing and rapidly changing economic and social reality, workers are now told to expect to change careers several times in a lifetime. This provocation toward

> To be wedded to work that is financially rewarding but little else is tragic. Shackles are shackles, even if they happen to be made of gold.

with God. Could it be that God has chosen to let us choose our purpose in order to intensify God's own delight?

As I write this, our third child, Joya, is deciding her college choice. Because of her hard work and natural ability, she has a wealth of options before her. I do not know what she will decide regarding school or choice of a major. As I think about it, I wouldn't want to know. I am, along with my wife and daughter, enjoying the process of deciding, the scared not-knowing, the "all things are still possible" stage of it all. A great joy of parenting is anticipation, waiting to see how thing are going to turn out. (Have you ever noticed that the words *sacred* and *scared* are spelled with the same letters?)

A third problem with the question "What is God's will for my life?" is that it leaves no room for human desire. Presenting God's will as the *only* influence flies in the face of the dialogical God we discussed earlier. It tends to promote God as puppeteer, not God as loving parent deeply interested in our free growth and free choice. Why would God give us creative freedom and then deny us the ability to use it in a matter as meaningful as our creative vocational expression and offering? Failing to allow for freedom in constructing the question of God's will in your life almost guarantees that human freedom will not be a factor in answering the question. The question unintentionally denies access to what I believe is the most important factor in vocational discerning, the divinely inspired desires of your heart.

Still yet another problem with this is that the last words are muted. For obvious reasons, "God's will" is bellowed; "my life" is often hushed. Yet it is *your* life. If God had wanted to, God might have enjoyed a humanless universe. However, God chose to create humanity, including you. It is vital that your "you-ness" be magnified, not diminished, in the expression of vocational fulfillment. As decreed by God, you-ness is no less sacred than God-ness. Indeed, our you-ness evolves from God-ness.

One of the holiest things you can do in the pilgrimage to discernment about vocation is give yourself a full hearing. Through silence, journaling, prayer, and other helps, you can befriend your authentic voice that expresses both your essence self and your evolving self—the self that was there from the beginning and will always be and the self that is ever-expanding and growing. The implication of this may be striking—maybe uncomfortably so—but that doesn't make it less valid: Vocational discernment is as much a matter of listening to you as it is listening to God.

Finally, the "God's will" question presupposes a fundamental not-knowing about vocation that may overshadow the process of getting clarity and ultimately doom it. Why must we believe that human purpose and divine will are things that must be found, searched out, or discovered? What if we were to imagine something different? What if we believed that sacred will and purpose were not at all hidden but ever before us? What if we believed that coming to clarity was not about looking harder elsewhere but looking more carefully at what was right in front of us? What if human purpose and divine will are less mysteries to be painstakingly decoded and more invitations and adventures to be delightfully accepted?

Demystify purpose, cease making it the hidden secret stored in God's hip pocket, and there is the possibility for vocational imagination and creativity the likes of which you have never dreamed of—until now.

Purpose and New Passions

Begin to think passion when you think purpose, and began to think bigger about passion. Presently, your confusion surrounding what to do or what to do *next* may stem from your not thinking broadly enough. For example, some of us automatically fit our vocational vision into the box of a favored familial career or job. You may become a teacher not because you really want to but because it's what many members of your family have done.

Or you may believe that the work has to be related to something you are already familiar with, a skill you have mastered. It is possible to select a vocation that will allow us to cultivate new skills and talents. The question "What am I good at?" may silence your hearing an even more amazing inquiry: "What hidden greatness is there residing inside me, dormant from my youth?"

Maybe the most common way we narrow our options is believing that what we are presently doing is what we should be doing for the rest of our lives, for financial reasons if no other. Though certainly not true in all cases, the greater the level of mastery, the higher the salary. That's what makes it dangerous to link vocational aspiration to financial situation so tightly that it obscures all other options. To be

change may be disturbing to some people, but I find it working on our behalf. This need to change is helping replace a
perspective that the fulfilled life is one in which one or two
vocational pursuits suffice. Many Christians believe that God
wills it so, that God has placed inside of us the kernel for one
or two vocational aspirations. So we had better find them or
run the risk of not fulfilling God's perfect will.

Holding a view that our true calling is limited to one
or two possibilities in today's altered work environment is
damning. What do you do when the one thing you feel
called to do is no longer an option? This is a layered problem—the problem of a lost vocation and the problem of a
closed mind, unable to conjure alternative possibilities. On
the other hand, with a mind-set that allows for the possibility of new passions throughout our lives, we are better suited not merely to survive but to thrive in a more volatile and
changeable work environment.

Jesus and Changing Passions

One of the greatest exemplars of passion and purpose was
Jesus. Most theologians would have you think that his singular purpose in life was serving as the world's savior.
Though that may have been his climactic purpose and the
one most revered by others, it was not his only purpose or
passion. According to the Gospels, his life is filled from
beginning to end with an assortment of passions that he
lived in the company of and in loyalty to his Father. Under

the tutelage of his earthly and often forgotten parent, Joseph, he enjoyed carpentry for the greater portion of his life. It wasn't until his thirtieth year that he took to teaching, that he allowed himself to feel the fires of a different calling, a new passion in his life.

To be sure, this is passion that had remained dormant inside of him; but it was there. Remember the story of Jesus as a child being intrigued by the teaching going on in the temple. He was so caught up in the burning of learning that he forget to meet his parents at the appointed time and was left behind. The teacher was in him earlier on, even as he was thoroughly absorbed with the artistry and precision of carpentry.

Carpenter, teacher—and Jesus still wasn't done. Bowing to the compassion welling up inside him, he became a healer. It was a new calling and passion that I am sure thrilled Jesus wildly, filling him with novel joy.

I once had a vivid dream in which I was sitting next to a dear loved one who was lying in a hospital bed. He could not move; somehow he had become paralyzed. I remember, in the dream, drawing close to this person, feeling his anguish, and responding with deep compassion and a desire for the condition to be altered in someway. That's all I did, express a silent desire from the depths of my heart that things would be different. I can remember feeling this as deeply as I could possibly feel anything. Then something extraordinary happened: My loved one suddenly sat up, threw the sheets off himself, got out of the bed, and started walking. I remember catching up with him and walking together with pure exaltation past the nurses' station.

My dream allowed me to feel some of the joy Jesus must have felt as he leaned into his new healing passion. I imagine him freely adding it to his expanding repertoire of vocational purposes and passions, because every time he healed, he too was healed in fresh new ways.

Still, Jesus remained open. Soon, as others flocked to him and some remained with him, Jesus became a beloved spiritual mentor. Anyone who has ever been a mentor knows that it is no small task. True mentoring is an art that stretches communicative and relational powers. The best mentors know that talking is a small part of the job; the larger part is listening and noticing, both of which take patience and time. Somehow, though challenged by increasing demands on him, Jesus chose to embark on yet another new vocational adventure, one that to be sure supported his healing and teaching work but opened up new avenues of challenge and fulfillment as well.

Toward the end of his life, Jesus assumed the role that for many believers is the most important, that of suffering servant. It may be said that this passion of Jesus was made possible though his fulfilling prior passions. One passion after the other grew him, opened him, widened him so that he was able to conceive and carry out a sacrifice that many of us would have declined if we could perceive it at all in the first place.

And according to the biblical record, Calvary was not the end of it for Jesus. There was yet another passion or purpose that Jesus was called to: resurrected Lord. This was the most stunning and striking purpose of all, in that it was radically different from any other calling he or anyone else had ever pursued before. If you believe in the resurrection of Jesus, I invite you as well to embrace its implication for moving from one summit to the next summit in our lives. Multiple purposes, passions, and desires are not the exception or the domain of the talented few but rather the open possibility for most, if not all, of us.

The key for Jesus and for us is our ability to imagine new possibilities for ourselves, especially possibilities that we may be tempted to rule out for one reason or another. We need to be able to see things that may have nothing to do with anything we have done before. Jesus lived one meaningful purpose after the other because he imagined these things in his mind and heart. To interpret imagination as the engine of our passions is not to do away with the notion of God calling us but to suggest that God may call us most often through our imagination, through our ability to perceive and envision new ways of being. His magnificent, albeit brief, life is characterized by a continuing willingness to follow different desires as those desires welled up inside of him. We would do well to think of his cumulative offering to humanity not just in terms of the passion or suffering of Christ but also in terms of the deeply and widely lived purposes of Christ.

Purpose Beyond Success

Odd as it may seem, we can miss the full blossoming of our purpose in life if we succumb to the sustained success of something we do very well. Phillip Moffitt, a noted magazine and software publisher, writes about the temptation and tragedy of limiting ourselves in this way: "The resistance to change in one's life when you're successful is incredible. It means giving up something known, to take the chance of achieving something unknown that will provide greater satisfaction. This resistance is why most people only change their life as a result of failure. That's really unfortunate. Life is so short and offers such diversity that repeating anything for a lifetime, no matter how successful, is ultimately a failure in imagination."

I am inclined to believe this. It's not that God doesn't call us to more; it's that we don't give ourselves permission to believe that God may be calling us to more through the budding of new passions. Our view of purpose is stuck in the mud of singular ordained pursuit and established skills and competencies. But we can regard purpose differently, in ways that stretch and ignite life in dynamic new ways. We open up amazing new pathways for ourselves with an understanding that does not link purpose tightly to the things we are good at. When we view purpose exclusively as the expression of our strengths, we miss the value of purpose as a sacred vehicle for exploring new abilities and powers.

I am not contending that each of us needs to have many different careers to experience fulfillment. The point is about living openly and possessing an experimental disposition about any work we find ourselves engaged in. The important thing is not to limit the full blossoming of our purpose in any way, even if we choose to remain in one career for life. A painter by the name of Hokusai offers a marvelous witness to this possibility:

Ever since the age of six I have had a mania for
drawing the forms of objects. Towards the age of
fifty I published a very large number of drawings,
but I am dissatisfied with everything which I produced before the age of seventy. It was at the age of
seventy-three I nearly mastered the real nature and
form of birds, fish, plants, etcetera.

Consequently, at the age of eighty, I shall have
got to the bottom of things; at one hundred I shall
have attained a decidedly higher level which I cannot define, and at the age of one hundred and ten
every dot and every line from brush will be alive. I
call on those who may live as long as I to see if I
keep my word.

Cultivating a Changing Mind

One day, I entered my office to continue my work on this
manuscript. Entering the completely dark room, I reached
for the switch on a light next to the desk. I did this for a few
moments without success. Then I realized something vital-
ly important. The light was no longer where I was reaching.
In fact, I had moved that lamp up to our youngest daughter's room months earlier. I had a new light on my desk.
Though I had long since grown accustomed to my new
light, in that moment I reverted to an old tendency. Though
I had placed a new lamp on my desk, I was still reaching for
the old lamp in my mind.

We have been discussing some fairly radical changes
from the way we have traditionally been taught to think

about purpose. In place of thinking that purpose is something preordained and set by God, I have asked you to consider that purpose is sacredly unsettled, that God leaves it to us to define our purpose as we are inspired by the Holy Spirit. And I have asked you to consider that purpose is not a singular calling, a hit-or-miss sacred best-case scenario for life. Rather, purpose is the sum total of a vast assortment of life challenges and possibilities that we have the potential to fulfill in our lives. Purpose is not closed but open. Purpose is not one thing but many things.

I hope you find these views liberating. I hope you are freed to think in more open ways about what you can do in life. I hope you are relieved of the tension and frustration associated with thinking that if you do this or that, you may not be observing God's perfect will for your life. In the end, that approach is a self-imposed restriction that may very well keep you from filling the desires of your heart—God's genuine primary intention for you

Seven Essential Benefits

Here are what I believe to be seven essential benefits of an open and broader understanding of purpose.

1. *We are inspired to consider more vocational opportunities when we consider our destiny to be open.* As long as we believe that we are called to do one thing in life, we will focus solely on that one thing. We see what we see. Our conscious and unconscious assumptions are responsible for what we see.

Once we become open to more, we have the possibility of experiencing more. If I had continued to see myself as a preacher and a preacher only, I would never have experienced the joyful pursuits of teaching and writing.

One of Jesus' biggest contributions was his vision of a broadened human possibility. He saw healing where others just saw sickness. He saw plenty where others saw need. He saw new life where others saw death. He saw the kingdom of God where others saw divisive parochialism. We have been fixated on what Jesus said and did; perhaps we need to spend more time pondering what he saw, his vision, and even more important, the divine creative act of imaginative envisioning open to us all.

2. *We are less filled with life-diminishing fears when we interpret God's will as an invitation, not a demand.* Once I greeted a couple whom I had not seen since their new baby girl was born. As the mother let me hold the baby, she prepared me by saying, "She doesn't do well with strangers and may start crying." I held this precious child and was thrilled by her presence. She didn't cry! As we looked into each other's eyes, we seemed engaged in a wondering contest with each other. But she was not afraid of me.

One of the greatest faults of institutional religion is that too often it has made us afraid of God. Adding this basic fear to the understanding that "God has something for you to do and you had better find out what it is," and you have a formula for living dysfunction.

It is possible to interpret God's will in no less respectful but more open and inviting ways. As with Moses, Mary, and Jesus, God is open to dialogue with us about our purpose in the world, even when God has strong suggestions of God's own. We are never made to do anything or to think that if we don't do this or that we have committed an unpardonable sin. In keeping with God's spirit of freedom and unconditional love and grace, God invites us to life. With a universe diverse and expansive as ours, is it not more natural to interpret purpose in diverse and expansive ways?

3. *We are better able to enjoy the gifts of imagination and creativity because we envision God valuing such things in the purpose-making enterprise.* In something as important as manifesting our life's work, why would God deny the expression of human creativity and imagination? If purpose is understood as something etched in stone, not to be altered, simply lived, our impulses toward imagination and creativity are hushed. I believe, however, that these traits are meant be celebrated in every dimension of life, including conceptualizing and acting out our purpose.

As I write this, the morning sun is shining trough the leafless trees in an astounding way. As I gaze out my window at the brightness of it all, I detect no inhibition whatsoever from the sun as it illuminates the branched forest. It is shining in full splendor. When it comes to human creativity and imagination, we tend to diminish them as innately spiritual realities. Creative and imaginative energy emanates from God. This innate energy is a part of who we are as children of God. Embracing it without restriction or limitation causes new ideas and possibilities to simmer inside, producing countless living dreams and possibilities.

4. *We are likely to experience job transitions less as a negative experience and more as an opportunity to explore our broader purpose.* New realities that lessen job stability may be daunting, but that may be less the case if we perceive ourselves to be possessors of enormous strengths—not just innate gifts, but the potential to grow new skills as we are inspired to do so by curiosity and necessity. Moreover, as we allow ourselves to think that changing vocational reality is the sacred norm and expectation, we can lean into transition when it comes.

Purpose is not one single best course consisting of elements that constitute our best ability; purpose is the sum total of everything that derives from innate strengths and evolving abilities. It's not just a matter of hearing a call once in a lifetime but hearing calls throughout our lives, all the while learning and growing.

> In something as important as manifesting our life's work, why would God deny the expression of human creativity and imagination?

One never knows where the next calling will be or what it will draw out of us. Rather than being an imposition, change is the great emancipator. I have a picture of a tree in my office. If you look at it from one angle, the tree is in full leaf. Look at it from another angle, and the leaves redden. From still another angle, the tree's limbs are covered in snow. A fourth angle shows a tree without any leaves. The title of the portrait is *Change.* We can choose to look at change not as abrupt interruptions that bring undue stress but as the inevitable grace of life that it is. This grace inspires new ways of seeing, being, and journeying. Without change, we would not leave the city limits of the familiar and would constantly be mistaking our universe for *the* universe.

5. *We place ourselves in a position to offer different gifts to the world and discover different and new skills in ourselves.* An expanded notion of purpose is not something that just does you some good. In a world filled with complexity and challenge, there has never been a time when a greater assortment and constellation of gifts has been needed. To meet the demand for fresh solutions, we all need to commit to freshness in living, to ride the unsettling wave of change in the world, because we are unafraid to ride the unsettling wave of change in our own lives.

Our ever-changing, pluralistic world thirsts for the creative juices of those who are filled to the brim with difference: different ideas and visions of what life can be. Their capacity for holding difference more than matches the nuanced layers of challenges the world presents to us. A stagnant and staid vision of oneself is the last thing the world needs to transform itself over and over again and thereby fulfill God's original and continuing intention for creation.

Rather than being an imposition, change is the great emancipator.

6. *We feel less obliged to continue in a vocation that has lost its appeal and excitement.* Many of us remain in a job simply because we can and because we earn a good living doing so. Such persons can stand doing the same things over and over again because they have mastered the steps and appreciate the stability. They can handle the periodic longing for something more and different because at least they are working.

Many of us have gown so accustomed to the dreariness of settling for less than we desire that we assume such gloominess to be the norm, indeed, the only genuine possibility. It is not. There are persons so in love with what they do that they can hardly wait to bound out of bed each day to return to their creative endeavor. In his book *Life Work*, Donald Hall states, "I leap out of bed. . . . I feel work-excitement building, joy pressure mounting—until I need to resist no more but sit at the desk and open the folder that holds the day's beginning, its desire and its hope."

My favorite work-joy testimony is from the jazz saxophonist Benny Golson, who once exclaimed of his experience, "Oh, it was so fertile, man! Every day was an adventure. We wanted to sleep fast so we could wake up and [start again]." Any perspective, theological or otherwise, that does not allow for such work-joy is sadly insufficient. One that directly disavows such feelings for vocation is down right sinful.

7. *We free ourselves to experience multiple vocational adventures throughout our lives.* Even if we don't want to, sociological and physiological factors are prompting us to prepare to be involved in various walks of life. Organizations can no longer be counted on to occupy a person for a twenty- or

thirty-year career, and most if us will be living longer than our parents, into our eighties and nineties. We would do well to prepare for the blessing of extended life by doing our part to ensure that these additional years are experienced as a blessing and not a burden. Developing a multiple-career mind-set helps us mentally prepare for the opportunities that will present themselves and even to be imaginative enough to create our own opportunities.

Beyond the Blinding Light

My hopes notwithstanding, hearing the views I have just espoused may have just the opposite effect that I intend. It is possible to perceive fabulous freedom as a glaring light. Knowing for the first time that we, as deemed by God, have a larger role in choosing our purpose and that such a purpose may change over a lifetime may be too much to take.

Once, when I was preparing to play a video game with my godson, Anthony, and explaining the game to him, he kept interrupting to ask for a joystick. Finally, I gave in and let him have it and plunge right in. Quickly overcome by the demands of a game he did not understand, he pushed the game controller back into my hand and said, "Here, you take it." In a similar way, we may feel overly burdened by the notion that purpose is open and multifaceted, that it has as much to do with what we really want as it does with what God really wants. In other words, we are unable to command the joystick in a meaningful way.

Something else that comes to mind is a comic strip I remember seeing. The first frame shows an egg at the side of the road. In the second frame, the egg begins to crack. The third frame illustrates the emergence of a little chicken. In the next picture, you can see that the bird has binoculars hanging from its skinny neck. Next, the bird is peering through the binoculars at its surroundings. The last and most memorable images are of the bird tossing he binoculars high into the air and then trying to get back into its shell. Whatever the chicken saw—or could no longer see—was too overwhelming.

If you are the least bit overwhelmed by thinking about purpose in a more open and varied manner, take a deep breath and choose to hold the tension of the new ideas. Don't abandon these new ideas for the comfort of familiar musings. Remember, if your prior thoughts and attitudes about purpose were all that you needed, you would not have picked up this book.

Besides, there is another step you must undertake that will make your new perspectives on purpose appear more as a brilliant star than a blinding light. Once you begin to see yourself in a new way, the light of purpose will appear as nothing more or less than the glorious and grand invitation God means for it to be. The first step to living your sacred purpose is seeing God and God's will in new ways; the second step is envisioning yourself in new way. Mark Twain once pointed out that the difference between the right word and the almost right word is the difference between lightning and a lightning bug. The difference between the right and the almost right perspective of who you are is just as dramatic.

EXERCISES

1. Have a dialogue with yourself as you answer the following questions. What have you set yourself up to see? In what ways have you limited your experience by limiting your perception? One way to see wide again is to return to the images you had of your grown-up self when you were a child. What could you see for yourself prior to the limiting conditioning of society? What could you imagine late at night when everything was dark? Did things you imagined seem as real as, if not more real than, reality itself?

2. Complete the following sentences in your journal.
    "My definition of purpose prior to reading this chapter was . . ."
    "My new definition of purpose is . . ."
    "My new definition of purpose excites me because . . ."
    "My new definition of purpose has me concerned because . . ."

3. Imagine that you have $15 million in the bank and ten years to live. What do you stop doing? What do you start doing? (Be careful not to fixate on how you would use the money. The point is that you are free to do what you will without being concerned about money.)

4. Draft an imaginary letter from God to you, incorporating some of the ideas discussed in this chapter. In the letter, God is challenging you to take more responsibility for your purpose, to search your desires and passions and engage

God in conversation. The goal is that you will conceive
and experience purpose as God's inspired invitation, not
God's closed demand. Read your draft over several
times. Pay attention to the new aspirations it brings forth
inside you.

6

not just creature but creator

One of my favorite movies of 2006 was titled *Akeelah and the Bee*. It is the story of a young girl who struggles against emotional, familial, and social barriers to win the National Spelling Bee. What a sheer marvel it is to watch Akeelah's transition from battered victim to bold victor! You can see the flame of self-awareness and confidence flare up inside her and burn brighter and brighter until family, neighborhood supporters, and amazed television viewers (and moviegoers) are all caught up in heartwarming inspiration. By the way, Akeelah's name is derived from a Swahili word for "intelligent person; one who reasons." Akeelah's mental trek is not just a journey into the challenging world of word origination and construction; it is an adventure into self-knowledge.

What we believe, including what we believe about ourselves, dictates who we are in this life. To a large extent,

> To a large extent, you are not who you are; you are who you believe you are.

you are not who you are; you are who you believe you are. When it comes to discerning and manifesting purpose in more magnificent and meaningful ways, we have some mental reformation to do. We are systematically conditioned to believe that we are less than we are. The sad fact is that many of the messages that diminish us are transmitted in the halls of religion, in the songs we sing, the prayers we pray, and the sermons we hear.

Before we discuss the primary idea of this chapter, conceiving and being more freely and fully our creator selves, I need to address a related matter, directly connected to our capacity to perceive ourselves as cocreators with God.

Worship and Human "Worthship"

I am writing something for the first time that I have suspected for some time. Much of what transpires in Christian worship unwittingly contributes to a view of persons as being less than we actually are in the eyes of God. In some church traditions, it is possible to be referred to as "a worm," "a wretch undone," "a sinner," and a besmirched person who needs to be "washed white as snow"—all in the same service. If you were down on yourself before worship, you really are in dire straits after worship service. Weekly rinses in this stream of messages—sometimes even more frequently—contribute to a low estimation of selfhood at best and a damning denunciation at worst. That such negative valuations of selfhood are rendered with biblical and theological endorsement adds to their potency. So it is that all too often a designated time of inspiration becomes in fact an occasion for inadvertent violation. When worship does not affirm human as well as divine worth, it has failed God and us.

Nowhere is God's disdain for dehumanizing worship more evident than in chapter 5 of the Old Testament book of Amos, where the portrayal of divine anger and indignation is unrestrained:

> I hate, I despise your feast days,
> And I do not savor your sacred assemblies.
> Though you offer Me burnt offerings
> and your grain offerings,
> I will not accept them,
> Nor will I regard you fattened peace offerings.
> Take away from Me the noise of your songs,
> For I will not hear the melody of your stringed
>   instruments.
> But let justice run down like water,
> And righteousness like a mighty stream.

Why is God so angry? Are the choir robes dirty? Has the preacher delivered a bad sermon? Is the offering too meager? No to all of the above. God's wrath is stirred by worship devoid of human concern and compassion. God is angry because worshipers have created a disconnect between making melody (worship) and making justice.

God does not need our honor and praise as much as God wants us to be inspired to see the honorable and praise-worthy inside of ourselves and others. Worship that diminishes God's creation in any way cannot be said to be praise to God. The question is not so much about what God receives from worship but about what you receive. Is your spirit buoyed, or is it battered? Are you encouraged to live on a higher plane, or have you just appeased yourself temporarily by having an emotionally high and scintillating religious experience?

> Any practice or thought that drags humanity through the mud of self-debasement cannot be said to be holy.

I have an overriding concern for how the human psyche is helped and hurt by religious practice. Any practice or thought that drags humanity through the mud of self-debasement cannot be said to be holy. Good religion celebrates God and God's creation, including selfhood. With all due respect to lifting God up, if your worship does not lift you up, does not let you know that you were made to soar, you have every reason to question and transform it.

Jesus and "Sinners"

Looking back on the life of Jesus, I am struck by one thing in particular, his unabashed noticing of "sinners," people who were far, far away from God. And it wasn't just that he noticed them but how he noticed them: with deep compassion. He loved them. His attentiveness to the religiously impure and socially unacceptable, to the least, the last, and the lost, was evident in his daily interactions. One minute he was sitting next to a woman at a well who was known for her sexual promiscuity; the next he was hollering greetings to a man perched in a tree who was regarded as one of the biggest embezzlers in town. The next day you could find him in an impromptu street court session taking the side of the accused, who had allegedly been caught in adultery. If you didn't know any better, you would think that this man of God preferred being with people who were far, far away from God.

This is exactly the point: Jesus didn't perceive them or anyone else, for that matter, to be far, far away from God. His signature contribution to the annals of religious learning was his focus on our *closeness* to God, not our distance from God. His insistence that the kingdom of God was within people regardless of their designated religious or socioeconomic status still stands as one the most striking and compelling beacons of light that any religious tradition has offered the world. He remained true to his belief to the point of death when some of his last drops of heartfelt concern are expressed not just toward his mother and associates but even to the people who are killing him, "who know not what they do."

What inspired Jesus to believe that each person was not far from God, from the grace and love of God? One way of explaining it is to accept as truth that Jesus was the ultimate human expression of God's love and as such knew its depth and reach in as fine and full a way as anyone has ever known it. How else can you explain loyalty to love to the point of death on the cross? He was convinced of love's ultimate supremacy.

I think he knew something else about love. He knew that all of creation emanated from it, including broken and estranged humanity. Thus no one could ever be far away from God, because the love of God was always in them, no matter how diminished or dormant. It was still there. Jesus never looked at anyone without seeing the mark of God's love in them.

Often my mother, Ora Mae Jones, who came to live with us after Hurricane Katrina devastated her home in New Orleans, will look at me and marvel at how much I look like one or another of my brothers. At eighty-nine, she finds joy in noticing and reveling in the marks. Jesus never saw anyone without seeing the mark, the mark of God's touch and God's love, which birthed life in the first place. He was not calling people to something new; he was calling them to observe their inner, albeit hidden, precious essence. Though many ended up embracing him, and still do, for Jesus that was the second embracing. The first embracing, and the one that mattered to him most, was that persons embrace their own divinity, the God-ness that was already in them and that could not be taken away by others' actions or designations.

Jesus' ministry was not challenging people to be righteous according to some doctrine or hierarchy. In his noticing all, Jesus invited all to notice themselves and to lean into being who they already were. In his mind, people did not have to become something; people simply had to be who they were in the full, free acceptance of God's unconditional love. The implication is unmistakable. In stark contrast to much of the teaching that has gone on in his name, Jesus had an extremely high estimation of humanness. Sin was the problem, never humanity. In his mind, human beings were esteemed and valued, from the cradle to the grave.

The Mark and Making Your Mark: Esteem and Creativity

Having someone affirm the mark of God on you is a powerful gift. When that happens, you start affirming it too, and you begin living the belief naturally. The energy created by such a deep and abiding affirmation is limitless. Such astounding living energy derives from the power of God's love and joyful confidence that is the result of living deeply affirmed.

When he was growing up in Washington, D.C., Duke Ellington's mother told him that he was "special," that he was "blessed." He recalled growing up believing that he was "God's son." Ellington grew up to become one of the greatest musical artists ever. He is as good an example as anyone of a magnificent link: the connection between esteem and creativity.

When we make that link, we feel more empowered to cocreate our lives with God. As we are able to affirm our essential worth and connection to God, we are better able to receive and embrace more fully the natural benefits that flow from union with the Divine.

Love, many people would suggest, is the most important gift we have as children of God. As God is love, and we are expressions of that love, we have the capacity to love in great abundance—though it may be argued that we have yet to scratch the surface in regard to sharing that love with persons outside our circle of preferred family and friends. If love is the greatest element in our spiritual DNA, the second is creativity, a trait also near the heart of God's essence. It would be as impossible to perceive of God without creativity as it would be to perceive of God without love. Creativity is at the very heart of God's nature and therefore an innate part of us, as God's creation, whether we realize it or not.

More Than a Buzz Word

The headline in the Sunday business section of the *New York Times* was striking: "The New Race May Be for Creativity, Not Speed." The article detailed the struggle by Intel Corporation to move beyond thinking that all that customers were seeking was faster and more powerful computer chips. Consumers were in fact interested in smarter computers, computers with built-in WiFi chips that eliminated the need to add such hardware later.

The article's implications, as far as I was concerned, went far beyond computer chips. Creativity over speed spoke to me of prioritizing new ideas, in general, over processing information and products as swiftly as possible. Just a few years ago, business gurus had declared that a company's profits and viability would hinge on adapting quickly to rapid-fire change. Now it's not how fast you know anything; it's the substance (the initial and continuing value) of what you know that really matters. Insight and sustainability are more important than speed. In the end, what we create matters more than how fast we receive information and disseminate products, including computer chips.

The following observation by Jennifer Ebert highlights the growing prominence of creativity in the business world:

> The most innovative companies consider creativity
> a value, but most organizations haven't begun to
> tap its potential. Few have embraced the power of

creativity and total reinvention. Yet we're beginning
to see the undercurrents of bold possibilities. We're
seeing signs of a new era where creativity drives the
bottom line. Where business escapes tradition and
embraces new practices that nurture and develop the
cultural creative mindset. Before long, these uncom-
mon approaches will simply be "business as usual."
Get ready.

Creativity is on the minds of many people, not just
those in the business world. Based on an increasing number
of books that have addressed the topic in recent years and
increased curiosity about it, there is a sense of humanity
having struck gold. Researchers in psychology, sociology,
anthropology, and neuroscience are involved in discussing
the essence, source, and characteristics of creativity, including such nuggets as curiosity, love of experimentation, playfulness, risk taking, and mental flexibility.

Though there is much more to discover about creativity, some conclusions are firmly established:

- We begin our young lives as "creative engines," but
  through an overemphasis on solving problems correctly
  in our schools, our experimental inclinations get taught
  out of us.
- One of the most important ingredients of creativity is
  relaxation and leisurely pursuits. Rigorous mental focusing must be balanced with emotional release to allow the
  mind to rest and release new insights.
- Geniuses and artists do not have a monopoly on creativity. We use our creativity every day to resolve matters as

mundane as rerouting ourselves away from a traffic jam or organizing our day in such a way as to provide for maximum productivity. Minds that can resolve those mundane matters in creative ways can be freed to address grander issues, too.

- Creativity involves having many ideas, including some bad ones. One cannot practice creativity fully and be afraid of failure. Put another way, those who fully embrace creativity know that there really is no such thing as "failure" since every outcome involves learning of some sort. A breakthrough may be defined as the sum total of learning achievements, including so-called failures.
- Collaboration breeds creativity. Even solitary creators such as scholars and writers read constantly and communicate with one another. Creativity may be at its best when people converge from different fields of study and expertise.

Creativity has reached such heights in our culture that some people have come to speak of a "creative class." Richard Florida sees this group as consisting of an inner core of people, such as scientists, engineers, and artists, whose "economic function is to create new ideas, new technology, and/or new creative content." Florida envisions an outer core or broader group of creative professionals in business, health care, and related fields who regularly engage in complex problem solving but not in fields we normally think of as being "creative." Both the core and outer-core creative types "share a common creative ethos that values creativity, individuality, difference, and merit."

On the whole, I am excited about the attention creativity is garnering. It coincides with my deepening appreciation for jazz music. Nowhere is creativity more valued and cultivated than in jazz. Indeed, I find it strange that more people writing about creativity don't turn to jazz as a huge historical carrier of creative energy and power.

It is important that we not assign creativity to any particular person or group—in other words, we must not place creativity exclusively in the hands or minds of a select few. Not only do we risk elitism, but we also are in danger of not noticing and valuing the creative spark that is in everyone in one form or another. For example, consider this enchanting exchange as recalled by Carolyn Dell'uomo:

> "Look! Look over there!"
> My black-haired, brown-eyed Mexican seat-mate
> nearly flew from her seat with excitement.
> "It's an angel riding a dragon across the sky!"
> I looked. I peered. I squinted. I put my glasses on
> and took my glasses off. Try as I might that dragon
> and rider eluded me. My six-year-old sage, Francesca,
> leaned forward and looked me straight in the eye. Her
> gaze potent with innocence and uncluttered wisdom
> was like a shaft of bright sunlight penetrating my
> overworked brain. She lay her soft brown hand on
> mine and with patient reassurance counseled me,
> "Don't try so hard. Sit back. Soften your eyes. Believe
> in them. Anything can happen now. You'll see."
> Following her guidance, I stopped trying to see. I
> peered out the plane's window, now beading with

tiny jewels of vapor, as we started our descent into Albuquerque.

My eyelids rested at half-mast, like those of a wise old mare patiently waiting for the supper bucket. Then I saw it. It came out of a cumulus cloud just as the captain announced the local weather. Like a proud student who had mastered her lessons I excitedly turned to my young mentor.

"I see a wiz . . ."

"Wizard!" she finished for me. Her little girl giggle became ancient, echoing from a place of deep wisdom within her. "You see? I said you could do it!"

Writers working from Christian or other spiritual perspectives do well to engage the conversation about creativity already in progress. We need to increase our awareness of a creative humanity as opposed to a creative class. This truth has monumental bearing for living our purpose. Living our purpose with ever-increasing confidence and imagination is integrally connected to our willingness to conceive and trust our role as cocreators with God.

Creativity and Spirituality

Writer and teacher Hal Zina Bennett writes, "Creativity is a sacred trust. And like all things sacred, it needs to be nurtured, respected, and heard in all its forms. It is through the expression of the creative spirit that humanity evolves and heals." Bennett's quote places creativity squarely in the realm of spirituality. The creative impulse is fundamentally a spiritual drive emanating from the heart of God. In his book In the Beginning . . . Creativity, Gordon Kaufman suggests that God's actions in the creation of the universe and the emergence of life are so dynamic and persistent that we would do well to see God as creativity and vice versa.

Biblical stories support the image of a God who fancifully produces and regularly expands the boundaries of possibility. In the Old Testament, a sea is turned to dry land, bread falls from the sky, trumpet blasts bring down walls, senior citizens become parents, a whale becomes a means of human transportation, humans survive in lion's dens and fiery furnaces, a heavenly hand sketches on a palace wall, and a flaming chariot soars in the sky.

In the New Testament, Jesus comes across as one of the most dynamically creative personalities of history. His parabolic method of teaching ingeniously meshed profundity with the stuff of everyday life. And then there were his spellbinding and mind-bending miracles. How dynamically creative is a person who changes water into wine, walks on water, halts storms, and raises the dead? Perhaps the most impressive evidence of Jesus' creativity was his ability to engender life in the

In the New Testament, Jesus comes across as one of the most dynamically creative personalities of history.

hearts and minds of his followers so that many of them later risked life and limb for his cause.

Highlighting the overwhelmingly creative nature of God and Jesus places the great Pentecost moment—the apostles' infusion with the Holy Spirit on the fiftieth day after Jesus rose from the grave—in a new light. The first followers were not just being filled with a spirit of love and courage to remain unified and carry on the mission in a volatile environment; they were being filled with an energizing agent that would enhance their every effort with love and courage. They were being filled with the life force responsible for creating and sustaining the universe. No wonder Jesus had told them before leaving them, "You will do even greater things than I have done." Jesus knew, even if they did not, that the Holy Spirit was not just a piece of Jesus but a fresh whole manifestation of divine energy. They were being filled with limitless creative energy that would constantly be meaningfully, if mysteriously, recharging itself inside of them.

> We are never more God-like than when we are expressing what makes God most God-like: loving, lavish, creative genius.

Spiritually speaking, creativity is the holy hallmark of everyone. It is nothing more or less than the power to imagine and actualize conditions and outcomes. It is the ability to express your life as you see fit. We are never more God-like than when we are expressing what makes God most God-like: loving, lavish, creative genius. Consequently, when it comes to faithfulness, it's not just how loving or long-suffering (perhaps the two most popular measures of spiritual growth) we are but how creative, in terms of leaning into our capacity to manifest life, we are. Creativity is not about art pieces; creativity is about your seeing your life as a piece of art and yourself as divinely inspired artist in residence.

What I am essentially asking you to do is revalue creativity. Bring it from the rear of the line to the very front in your thinking about God. Give creativity the highest rating you can possibly give it. When you think of God, don't just think the laudable traditional value of love, goodness, and justice; think creativity. Just as important, when you envision discipleship, change your standards. It's not just about your being a loving and sacrificial person; it's about your being someone who owns and appreciates the sacred power to imagine and creatively actualize what you imagine. Dare to believe even that more than a gift of the spirit; creativity is the Spirit.

Creativity and Purpose

Buoyed by a new understanding of our creative empowerment, we can look at purpose in a striking new way: Purpose is not something that we passively receive from God but something that we actively cocreate with God. You will not be overwhelmed by this as long as you remember who you are and the power residing inside you as a child of God. Rather than being paralyzed by the truth of your cocreator status, you should feel a new vitality in your bones and spirit. I believe it is what God would have us feel in the face of forging a vocational life. Don't be afraid; be thrilled, and use your powers.

The word *powers* may throw you. While many Christians are comfortable enough speaking about God's power and even the power of evil, they display a palpable resistance when it comes to speaking freely and positively about human power. Human power is perceived as automatically opposed to God's power. Nothing could be further from the truth. Power, creative energy, emanates from God. As such, it is energy that can be used for good or misused for evil.

God's power does not hinge on your powerlessness. To hear or observe some Christians, you would think that the more powerless you feel, the more faithful you are. To be sure, this is informed by long-standing theological assumptions about self-denial and meekness. But such realities themselves, in their truest manifestations, are forms of potent strength, not weakness.

To a large extent, coming into your own in every dimension of your life is a matter of learning to embrace and engage your power. Your ability to do so will determine your capacity to engage and not feel threatened by the power of others. You may be thinking, "This is beginning to sound like New Age philosophy or a Harry Potter book."

The fact is, you can find arguments about living in the fullness of our powers in the Bible:

> But those who wait on the Lord
> Shall renew their strength;
> They shall mount up with wings like eagles,
> They shall run and not be weary,
> They shall walk and not faint.
>
> *Isaiah* 40:31

> Behold, I send the Promise of My Father
> upon you; but tarry in the city of Jerusalem
> until you are endued with power from on high.
>
> *Luke* 24:49

> For God has not given us a spirit of fear
> but of power and of love and of a sound
> mind.
>
> *2 Timothy* 1:7

When you read of power like this in the Bible, no less, how does it make you feel? If you have been reared with a belief that reserves all power for God or one that focuses on the misuse of power to the point of identifying evil with power, you may be uncomfortable. But it is a creative discomfort. Initially, it may be uncomfortable to see power in a new light and in a way that can unleash dynamic new energy inside you. This is energy that can enhance every-

thing about you, from your
ability to imagine to your
capacity to exert your will
to your ability to actualize your desires regard-
ing anything, including
your purpose in life.

> Giving yourself
> permission to
> see yourself in an ever-
> empowering light is
> the key to living
> fulfillment and joy.

Giving yourself per-
mission to see yourself in an
ever-empowering light is the key
to living fulfillment and joy. If you can't see it, you can't
have it. Start imagining yourself the way a grand and gen-
erous God would. Moreover, perceive your enhanced
notion of your empowered self in the holiest of lights. Such
a view has nothing whatever to do with selfishness but
everything to do with sacred "selfness."

Accept Your Sacred Incredible

I have an old newspaper article about a local baseball play-
er who had just been drafted by a major league team. The
article is filled with accolades for this young pitcher: "He's
going to be in the big leagues," "He is a tremendous talent,"
"His stuff is already there." This young ace had a lot going
for him, but there was one glaring weakness: He had a control problem. At points during games, he would lose the
ability to throw a strike, sometimes missing the plate by a
wide margin. The reason for the pitcher's problem? One of

his coaches was sure that the solution was not a mechanical one, such as changing the pitcher's delivery or the way he held the ball. This coach was convinced that the problem was more mental than mechanical: "He's always been good, but he's never thought he was all that good. Once he believes in all his talent, he'll be unbelievable." That comment is the reason I kept the article.

How about you? Do you believe in all your God-given talent? In other words, can you humbly and gladly accept the sacred incredible in you, in particular, the creator in you?

EXERCISES
1. How would you have defined creativity before reading this chapter? How do you define creativity after having read the chapter?
2. What new thoughts about your purpose do you have, knowing that God *expects you* to use your creative genius in arriving at what you want to do in life?
3. Seat yourself comfortably and clear your mind. When your mind is clear, hear God say to you, "You have my blessing in whatever you want to do. What would you like to do?" Write down the first thoughts that enter your mind without editing or judging what you write. Once you've finished writing, survey your response for words and ideas that call forth the most energy inside you. Your elevated energy is an indicator of your God-blessed, heartfelt vocational desire. Receive God's grace by coming up with ways to live your desire.

4. Informed by the ideas set forth in this chapter, imagine a dialogue in which you and God are talking freely and openly about your purpose. Develop a transcript of the dialogue. Note the points where you say things to God you have never said before and you hear God say things to you that you've never heard before.

7

three great creative powers

Once, while on a ferry to Martha's Vineyard in Massachusetts, I noticed our youngest child, Jovanna, taking pictures of seagulls. I had no idea that I was witnessing a profound creative breakthrough. Years later, in a class presentation on her expanding photography hobby, Jovanna explained that it started when she dared to take pictures of one of her greatest fears: seagulls. She said, "I took them despite the fact that I thought they'd swoop down and eat my camera." Through daring and desire, Jovanna excerised one of her and your greatest powers: the power to create.

Our power to create is our supreme spiritual birthmark. Why wouldn't we have such a feature as the offspring of God, our loving creator? Our creativity is an awesome gift that allows us to feel life-giving energy, or what we traditionally refer to as "Holy Spirit." Freely using our creative power is an expression—maybe the highest expression—of living in the Spirit.

When it comes to creating your life purpose, you have three distinct but related abilities: the power to choose, the power to perceive multiple choices or options, and the power to create alternative choices.

The Power to Choose

Last year, I had an exchange with our now thirteen-year-old daughter Jovonna that stirred mixed emotions inside of me. I'd asked her to do a small favor. Her response was uncharacteristically cold and resistant. Assuming that fatigue was the cause, I informed her that I did not appreciate her stance and said that perhaps what she needed to do was to take a nap. That's when she said it: "No." I was momentarily stunned by the deliberate strength of her voice. In that moment, a part of me was saying, "How dare you!" But I was feeling something else as well. It wasn't just what Jovonna said but how she said it and how she looked at me when she said it. I did not observe disrespect in her; I saw an emerging insistent personality. I wanted to shake her and embrace her at the same time. Though incensed by her choice, I was impressed with her choosing.

Part of the gift of life is human choice.

In his classic book *Man's Search for Meaning*, Viktor Frankl writes the following words: "We who lived in concentration camps can remember the men who walked through the huts comforting others, giving away their last piece of bread. They may have been few in number, but they offer sufficient proof that everything can be taken from a man but one thing: the last of the human freedoms—to choose one's attitude in any given set of circumstances, to choose one's own way."

Our power to choose is hindered most, perhaps, by overly aggressive parenting, overfixating on the power of others over us, and the deluge of choices in our postmodern world. As we've discussed, for some Christians and some other spiritually minded people, our choices can be hindered by beliefs that life is a matter of discovering God's will, to the exclusion of any concern at all for one's own will, one's own God-endowed desires. So it is that some believers live constantly under the shadow of wondering whether or not their aspirations and actions are in accord with God's will. That can blind us to the fact that a part of the gift of life is human choice. It is not just about what God wills; it is about what we will, what we choose.

In my book *Addicted to Hurry: Spiritual Strategies for Slowing Down*, I imagined that God was fed up with our spiritualized sheepishness surrounding taking responsibility for our lives:

> The next time you turn something over to God or
> tell God to decide something for you, wait a
> moment. You may hear God say gently but firmly:
> *Deal with it. For my sake and yours, please deal with it. I am with*
> *you. I will help you, but dare to decide and live responsibly with*
> *the results of your choice. If I wanted to do it all by myself, I*
> *would not have created you in the first place, especially with all the*
> *abilities and gifts I have placed inside of you. Besides, I love to see*
> *you engaging challenges, creating possibilities, and choosing between*
> *options. I love watching you grow.*

Making choices is an integral part of breaking through to clarity about vocational pursuits. Not long ago, a ministerial friend called to ask my opinion regarding a vocational shift he'd been contemplating. A pastor for more than twenty-five years, he was now considering becoming a consultant to churches on matters related to communication technology. In fact, he had been consulting on the side for years; he was at the point of wanting to do this work full time. After hearing him go back and forth on whether or not he should move from pastoring to consulting, I told him what I frequently tell others who are betwixt and between and wanting some sense of vocational direction, especially about which way God is leading them. Here's a thought: Suppose God is not leading us anywhere but open to journeying where we, in God's freedom, are playfully desiring to go.

Remembering my own liberating experience on the banks of the Hudson River, I said, "Suppose God is telling you to choose. Suppose God is saying that whatever you decide, I will always be with you. Suppose God wants you to see how both paths—and maybe a few others—hold comparable potential for personal growth and meaningful offering to the world."

For a moment there was silence, followed by positive acceptance of a new way of perceiving God's role in our decision making. God is not the ultimate decider but rather the loving encourager. The choice is ours; the choice is mine and yours. Such is the angst and thrill of being alive, truly.

God wants to inspire and inform your vocational choices; God does not want to make such choices for you.

God wants to inspire and inform your vocational choices; God does not want to make such choices for you.

Embracing choice gives us freedom to explore a vast assortment of vocational alternatives. Released from a narrow, life-diminishing perspective of God's dominating will, we are free to consider new pursuits. Avenues previously walled off by a notion of God's not wanting us to do this or that are now wide open. The tension of discerning whether or not we are in God's will has been melted away by a new understanding: God's will is not the only will that matters; by God's own decree, your selective will matters too, if not most.

The Power to Perceive Multiple Options

In a prior chapter, we discussed the plethora of options in our world as a sometimes stressful challenge. It doesn't have to be that way. For example, it is a beautiful thing to be stuck in traffic and then realize that an alternative route is available to you at the next exit. As a preacher and teacher, I am thrilled by the knowledge that there are multiple ways of expressing a single truth. This adds to the fun and fulfillment of communicating effectively and creatively. More than cursed, we are blessed by options.

You are not limited to what you think God wants. Theologically speaking, your perception of God is necessarily smaller than God's reality. Therefore, your options will always be beyond your biggest perceptions of God. Moreover, as I have argued, God wants you to be free to explore your own interests and desires.

You are not limited to your perceived strengths and skills. We limit ourselves and our possibilities when we perceive good work as doing something we are accomplished and good at. Good labor may also be the flowering of a vocational strength or merely a vocational exploration, excellent for exploring's sake. The quality of the work is measured less by level of accomplishment and more by learning and development.

I suspect that we are all Renaissance souls when we come into the world, capable of many things, but very soon we lose our soul's vast abundance. We are socialized away from playful exploration and creative expression. We become convinced that how much we earn and whom we work for matters more than whether or not our soul is singing.

The Power to Create Choices

Your creative prowess does not stop at your capacity to discern and make multiple choices. The third layer or zone of your strength is the most potent and underused element. It is your capacity to create options, to develop opportunities that would not exist apart from your capacity to conceptualize and enact them. This is the power of carving a path where there is none, or as Isaiah hears God saying, "making a road in the wilderness and rivers in the desert" (Isaiah 43:19).

One sees this occurring over and over in the life of Jesus. He possessed an uncanny ability to concoct new options. For example, when a woman who is thought to be an adulteress is brought to him for his sure condemnation, Jesus neither joins her accusers nor condones her adultery. As he draws on the ground, he invents a third choice: putting her accusers on the defensive by saying, "Let him who is without sin cast the first stone." Seemingly backed into a corner of either violently condemning the woman through stoning or carelessly turning a deaf ear to the risks of adultery, Jesus perceived an alternative option. He saw and seized a way of enveloping all, not just the woman, in a spirit of wider and broader ethical accountability. He didn't take her off the hook; he put everyone on the hook, including himself.

Another example of Jesus' creative genius was his handling of a storm one night. As Jesus slept aboard a vessel, his disciples battled fear amid what Scripture calls a "tempest," a storm of hurricane intensity. When the sleeping Jesus is awakened, he joined his disciples. Perhaps the disciples felt that his presence alone would be sufficient to help them sail through the storm. Or maybe they believed that he would speak with them in such a way that they would no longer feel threatened by the storm. Whatever their expectations, chances are they did not foresee Jesus' doing what he did. Jesus began speaking to the storm. His effective "Peace be still" is another example of Jesus' ability to devise ways beyond those that are known and obvious.

What does this have to do with vocation? When it comes to discerning and deciding what you want to do, you need to prepare for the possibility that you may not know the "what." It may be that you will be inspired to either create the what by connecting different pieces (labor familiar to you) or devising it from scratch. Your calling may not be listed in the job search manuals. For the time being, it is listed only in your soul's inspiration, and the only way you will find it is to believe in what you are hearing and sensing.

Stirring Up Your Creativity

The primary message of this chapter—and much of this book—is that purpose is not something we discover, find, or receive; purpose is something that we cocreate with God. An awareness of our creative responsibility and power regarding purpose creates new energy and insight for making our purpose happen. But to ensure ongoing creativity in life in general and regarding your purpose in particular, let me suggest seven ways to stimulate your creativity.

1. Expect to Be Creative

More than anything else, we are limited by our expectations. Creativity is not the exclusive domain of the few we deem intelligent and artistic. It has to do with the openness and energy with which we engage and construct life. Notice your capacity to choose, perceive choices, and come up with alternative options in the mundane areas of your life, such as scheduling your day or shopping. Broaden your perception of your creative power to include your life and purpose. Imagine what it would be like if you allowed yourself to be fully creative in the way you perceived your purpose. Do this while excitedly expecting to conceive new ideas and possibilities, and you will create new possibilities more readily and easily.

I practice this expectation with writing. I realized some time back that the mind-set I brought to my writing influenced my writing session. Initially my goal was just to spot negative thinking and reject it. Then I began actively replacing negative thinking with alternative positive thoughts. Finally, I began filling my mind before each session with fabulously positive thoughts. Why not think fabulous thoughts, since our minds are going to be filled with something either way? One of the mental alternatives is fabulous positive thinking. Why not use it even more? Currently, I am writing after having filled my mind with this deceptively potent sentiment: "I am in a wonderland where words come easily, sentences flow freely, and thoughts and ideas abound! Oh, what fun! what play! what joy!" I know it sounds wild and whimsical, and it certainly doesn't take the arduous work out of writing. But it does cultivate a mindfulness that allows for playful labor. Playfulness unleashes energy and intuition, which are blocked by the perception of work as burdensome and laborious. Change your perception, and you change your experience.

Here is another sentiment I have embraced just before writing portions of this book: "I write playfully and bountifully with simmering passion and relaxed confidence." Expect to be creative. What do you have to lose? What do you have to loose?

2. Be Still

Much of our creative energy is dissipated in the constant bustle and rush of everyday life. Observing mental stillness regularly provides the openings for deeper reflection and clarity. In *What We Ache For: Creativity and the Unfolding of Your Soul*, Oriah Mountain Dreamer makes the following

observation: "If there is one consistent thing that stops people committed to doing creative work from doing it, it is
this: a lack of necessary silence in their lives, an inability or
unwillingness to find and stay with the stillness, to regularly create empty time in their day or their week." How many
times have you had the answer to a pressing concern just
pop into your head while you were casually involved in a
leisure task or resting? That was no accident. Your mind dis-
engaged and was free to roam in other places, places that
contained the solution you sought. This is not to say there
is no place for hard thinking, but hard thinking does not
hold a monopoly on creative insight. The mind in eased
stillness is a potent underused source of colossal creative
energy and insight. The only way you can discover this for
yourself is to dare to be still more often.

3. Listen to and Trust Your Inner Voice

Herbie Hancock, the brilliant jazz keyboardist, reflecting on
a period of creative unrest, wrote:

> By the end of 1972, my feeling was that the sextet
> had reached a peak, and it sustained that peak for a
> while, and we tried to go beyond that, but it was
> like fighting uphill. I suspected that my own energy
> needed something else. It was more spiritual, and it
> had more to do with me as a human being. I knew I
> didn't want to play the music I had been playing,
> but I didn't know what music I wanted to play. I
> hadn't quite figured it out. I wanted to find the
> answers within myself.

More than anything else, I am touched by Hancock's sens- ing that he needed to sub- merge inside himself in order to more clearly identify the next artistic summit. Hancock's expe- rience suggests that new heights are grasped through taking the time to journey within,

> It is one of the surest and simplest, albeit nonsensical, truths of all: The way up is down and in.

to touch our innermost callings. It is one of the surest and simplest, albeit nonsensical, truths of all: The way up is down and in.

4. Enjoy More Leisure

In *The Breakout Principle*, Herbert Benson and William Proctor suggest that the way to really be *on* is to be *off* more:

> To make your escape from the downward spiral into destructive stress, you can "back off," "let go," or "release" the pressure that is bearing down on you by switching on the breakout mechanism. As we have seen, that may mean soaking in a tub of water, taking a walk in the woods, listening to a Bach con- certo, or retreating in solitary prayer. . . .
>
> Pulling the breakout trigger in any of these ways will sever past patterns of thought and emotion. At the same time a series of helpful biochemical "explosions" will begin to bubble up inside your brain and body.

Of the various biochemical explosions Benson and Proctor highlight in their book, none is more vital than the leisure-induced release of nitric oxide, "message-carrying puffs of gas that course through the entire body and central nervous system." Among its fascinating wealth of offerings, nitric oxide enhances memory and learning by operating as a transmitter between brain synapses, increases the release of dopamine and endorphins, which promote a sense of well-being and help regulate blood flow throughout the body.

Going, going, going like the Energizer bunny is not only a serious health risk but also a sure way to diminish creative vitality.

5. Practice Holy Openness
(Sacred Not-Knowingness)

When Jesus said, "Except you become as a child, you cannot enter into the Kingdom," I believe he had more than heaven in mind. I think he had the realm of all-things-are-possible in mind. As children, our not-knowingness works for us more than it does against us. We would do well to cultivate a not-knowingness even as we become knowers. The not-knowing-ness about us is the thing that keeps us soft and flexible to possibilities that surety makes off limits. Not-knowing is far better than knowing all too well. The tragic consequences of the latter is captured in the following observation by the late, great American Baptist pastor Gene Bartlett:

> What surprises there are! We are such planners! We
> decide how God must come into human affairs. We

treat it all with a kind of public relations twist. We pick the time and the place. We insure that the right people are there to meet God. We get the news releases out as to what to expect. We even have some prepared quotes. But God has an uncanny way of taking care of times and places and entrances. While we wait at the airport, as it were, with a representative committee of dignitaries, an escort waiting for the coming, God has a way of quietly arriving at the bus station, walking up the side street, and slipping, unnoticed, through the servant's chambers.

The supremacy of not-knowing is confirmed in this poignant story recalled by noted Buddhist spiritual leader Thich Nhat Hanh:

The Buddha told a story about a merchant who everyday left his house, and his little boy remained at home. One day pirates and thieves came and robbed the house and burned it. When the merchant came back he saw the charred body of a child and believed it was his son who had died. He cried and beat his chest. He tore out his hair. He reproached himself for having left his child at home. And then he performed the funeral rites. He cremated the body of that child. And being so attached to the child, he carried the bag of ashes with him wherever he went. When he ate, he had the bag. When he worked, when he slept, always he had the bag with him. Then a few months later, the child, who had

been kidnapped by the pirates, was released. One
night, he got back to the house and knocked on the
door. "Father," he said, "I'm back." But the father
did not believe it. He believed his child had already
died. So he refused to open the door. And the child
finally had to go away.

You must desire and practice, in the words of the poet Mary
Oliver, "the openmindedness of not knowing enough about
anything."

6. Be Joyful

I had one of those living dreams; it seemed like I was actually there, at a celebration of Nelson Mandela's release from
prison. Mandela's liberation and subsequent ascent to the
presidency of South Africa was one of the truly great events
of the past century. It was a global occasion for joy. Yet at this
very festive celebration in my dream, I was not joyful. I
seemed distracted. At one point, I allowed my attention to be
drawn away from the festivities and onto an altercation
between two men, a disagreement they soon resolved on
their own. I awakened from the dream wondering why, with
joy all around me, I was not joyful. It dawned in me that
although I was surrounded by joy in my dream, I chose to
turn my focus away from it. I chose not to focus on the joy.

In part, observing joy is more a matter of raising our
joy threshold or limit. There is a curious malady that religious people seem to be especially susceptible to: They can
only take so much joy before beginning to feel guilt.

Somehow, we have been conditioned to believe that life is supposed to be more sorrowful than pleasurable. There are brands of Christianity that make somberness a virtue. Whatever the cause, we are challenged to raise our threshold for joy. What would it mean for us to take more truthfully the Gospel's glad good news of not just joy, but "great joy"?

> There is a curious malady that religious people seem to be especially susceptible to: They can only take so much joy before beginning to feel guilt.

I remember a dear friend's graduation day. More memorable than the day and the degree was the way she embraced it all. She gleamed as she marched in the procession and received her diploma, in her golden shoes. She shouted like a child on Christmas morning as we walked to the car to take her to dinner. She ordered her meal and ended by proclaiming to our waitress, "I just graduated!" While waiting for ice cream in the back seat of the car, she appeared to be basking in the glory of the day. And she noted aloud that because she had not been able to graduate with her high school class, this was her first real graduation. She spoke of now knowing that God had not forgotten her. She sat at our kitchen table at the close of the day and gazed toward her future, with visible joy.

What would it mean for you, in the words of Zora Neale Hurston, to "have a heart with room enough for every joy"? In this relentless spirit, we create not because we know how but because we can't help ourselves. Creativity is the overflow of a joyous soul.

7. Cultivate a Playful Heart

You are going to hear more about play in the final chapter of this book. But there is no leaving it out when it comes to suggestions about becoming more creative. If you don't play, you will not create. There can be no genuine, meaningful, and sustained creativity without play.

> Creativity is the overflow of a joyous soul.

You may have to address some negative opinions of play, which is often dismissed as detracting from necessary seriousness. In this way, we may accuse someone of "playing too much" and therefore needing to "grow up." Another way play is downgraded is by using the term in reference to dishonest behavior. We refer to unfaithful spouses as people who "play around." In some circles, persons having several intimate involvements simultaneously are regarded as "players."

These unfavorable meanings notwithstanding, play, pure and innocent, is one of the most powerful realities in the universe. When we play, we become absorbed in free engagements that challenge and broaden us and, just as important, bring us joy. This union of focus, adventure, and pleasure unleashes an anticipation for more of the same, initiating a cycle of an endless, at times breathless, sacred flow of abundant and creative life.

Creative persons often refer to their labor in playful terms. As the best-selling author Stephen King has observed, "Writing is at its best—always, always, always—when it is a kind of inspired play for the writer. I can write in cold blood if I have to, but like it best when it's fresh and almost too hot to handle. . . . When I'm writing, it's all the playground, and the worst three hours I ever spent there were still pretty damned good."

Watch Heaven Rejoice

As you embrace your self as cocreator with God, do so without any inhibition. The freer you are in doing so, the more energy you create for imagining and manifesting your destiny with God. I believe we have God's permission to plan and play our dreams and desires. Indeed, the following poem I was inspired to write says that God's great joy is our joyous self-expression and expansion.

> *Watch Heaven Rejoice*
> Can you stand
> living in light?
> Can you imagine
> sustained joy,
> sharpened intuition,

and expanded intelligence?
Can you wield
the sword of your own brilliance?
Answer, "Yes."
And watch heaven rejoice.

EXERCISES

1. Write a poem or short prose essay in which you affirm your divine creative powers.
2. Doodle an image of God empowering you to be your most creative self.
3. If you are having difficulty with the first two exercises, ask yourself why. What is blocking you from affirming your identity as cocreator with God?

8

dreaming your way to purpose

In what was the most vivid and involved daydream I ever had, I saw a cabin situated near a lake. Suddenly I felt myself within the small wooden structure. I was immediately struck by a sense of being trapped—each window was closed, and I sensed that all doors were locked shut. The room felt confined, stuffy, and increasingly uncomfortable. Then, suddenly, something truly amazing happened: I sensed a presence other than my own in the house. I was not afraid; I was awed. This presence, more spirit than flesh, began to whirl and twirl its way within the cabin. It went from one window to the next, flinging them all wide open. When all the windows were open, it exited through a doorway it designed with its own disappearance. The closed house on the lake had, in a holy magical moment, been transformed into a space of exuberant openness.

Though the daydream first arrived without my bidding or intention, I know I can call on it at will when I want to feel the fresh empowerment of open thoughts and perspectives. As I began to reflect on the main ideas I wished to convey in this chapter, the daydream returned to me with new understandings that matter immensely to dreaming and living our dreams. The dream, it seemed, had something to say to us about dreaming, about dreaming on purpose. This is the message I imagined the dream saying to me.

Dreams and Freedom

When the dream came to you, it was to set you free, to set your mind free to consider new alternatives for yourself, some you had never before given yourself permission to think. Remember, you were in the throes of vocational transition. One of your primary challenges was seeing beyond your set vision for yourself. All of your life, you saw yourself as a minister. But you should never see yourself one-dimensionally, no matter how laudable that dimension may be. The universe is simply too grand and glorious to fixate on singular images of your purpose—or anything else, for that matter. Just consider the vast variety of species of flowers, or rocks, or animals. God fancies difference.

Allowing yourself to think differently and freely about what you want to do in life is a great grace, one that God expects you to take full advantage of. Dreams are toys for constructing new truth. In dreams, you are not limited to known perceptions and prefer- ence. Dreams rain down imaginings that can inspire liberating new images of person- hood and purpose. They are life openers, making it possible for you to conceive what you never dared to imagine.

> Dreams are toys for constructing new truth.

Therefore, when dreams arrive, the best thing to do is to let them be, let them dance without restriction in the rooms and corridors of your mind. You'll never regret it. What dreams inspire in you from a place that knows no limitation will always surpass the offerings of your restrict- ed rational reasoning.

Dreams and Desire

It's a funny thing: When dreams arrive, they are often per- ceived as strange and unreal. In my dream of the house on the lake, I perceived the dream "me" as some unknown and mysterious entity. But in fact, it came from within me; it was the manifestation of my deepest desires. It wanted me to see myself in a new way, to pursue something that was different from what I had been doing for so long.

Yes, this is about desire. Why have so many people turned that into a bad word? How have we forgotten that wholesome desires are God's yearnings? Attend to what excites you naturally, what makes you smile by the energy of its being inside of you. We need never be suspicious of possibilities that spark our souls and minds. That spark is the Spirit calling forth the best, highest, and grandest we are capable of offering divinity and humanity.

Even daydreams are our deepest desires taking flight. Grounded by the restrictions of our rational minds, our limited view of what we think we are capable of, dreams flow where they can, in our imaginations, the fanciful seedbed of truly inspired and meaningful purpose.

Dreams and Excitement

Dreams come to us unbidden, but through memory we can choose to call them forth often. We are compelled to do so for one reason in particular: the way the spirit presence whirled and twirled, opening windows and doorways. It is not just the images of the dream that keep coming back to us but also the energy of it.

As you ponder purpose, pay attention to your energy highs and lows. What do you feel energized and excited about? What fills you with feelings of inspired interest? What calls forth joyful curiosity? What unleashes feelings inside you akin to those you had as a child when you were just having fun—when you were at holy play? Notice the vocational prospects that seem to have such power, the power to thrill you. They are calling you; let them. Feel the exuberance and the fire. Don't be afraid of being excited by dreams that delight you. Don't be afraid to commit to one delightful dream after another. Don't be afraid of dancing your dream with God. Your excited acceptance of your dream excites God. Excitement is a sign—one of the surest—of the Spirit's pleasure.

The Divinity of Dreaming

Great thinkers have mused on the power of dreams. "I freed my wings from the bonds of weakness and submission and rose in flight through the air of love and freedom," wrote the poet Kahlil Gibran. "In addition to my own intrinsic worth, I must find some movement or cause or purpose that is more significant than my own life. I must find something that gives some radical test for all that is highest and best in me," wrote Howard Thurman.

What makes your purpose divine is not so much that God is willing it but that you are, using your God-given capacity to dream and desire. God's thrill is that you intentionally and purposefully join God in the holy dream-play of life.

Dreaming, the capacity to imagine anything, is one of our most potent abilities. I have referred to imagination as the second most powerful force in the universe, second only to godly love. Think of any entity at all that is humanly constructed, and you will have to agree that before it was a physical construct, it was a mental one. From music to museums to monuments, we create through the power of imagination.

If you begin to really believe that God is your divine partner, that purpose is an open possibility, and that you are a creator, you will realize that you can dream not just a purpose but your widest and grandest purpose. Open and more spacious understandings of God, purpose, and personhood free us to dream in more open and spacious ways. In words attributed to Joseph Campbell, "It is the scope of the aspiration that matters." There is an integral link between small dreaming and small living. Through God's creative calling, the life we live is the life we call forth.

Dreaming Possibilities

The noted actress-singer Queen Latifah starred not long ago in a film titled *The Last Holiday*. It is about a sales associate in New Orleans who is mistakenly told that she has only a few weeks to live. The associate, played by Latifah, is emotionally decimated. But after episodes of hard and heart-wrenching grieving, she decides to use the time she thinks she has left to live some of her dreams, aspirations she has been collecting in a "possibilities book." Latifah's character ends up living her dreams and in the process inspires others to live theirs.

One of the lasting images I have from the movie is the possibilities book. In a way, it was more important than the hundreds of thousands of dollars she had saved to realize her dreams. With such limited time, it was good that Latifah's dreams had already been dreamed and chronicled. She didn't waste any time; she could move immediately toward making her long-held dreams a reality.

God has bestowed on us all the magnificent blessing of being able to dream dreams, to imagine anything and everything for ourselves. Whether or not we are able to or dare to, we can all dream anything we want. Why on earth would we think that the God who empowers us to dream would require that we dream limited and small dreams? Why wouldn't God want you to use your capacity to dream, to imagine your vocational pursuits and explorations in wide, even grand ways? Take the limits off of what you have been imagining for yourself. Allow yourself to dream like you have never dreamed before. Use the liberating energy of your new beliefs about God, self, and purpose to catapult you to new aspirations and desires.

Why on earth would we think that the God who empowers us to dream would require that we dream limited and small dreams?

Free to Dream on Your Own Terms

Once while taking an early morning walk in Philadelphia, I came across a striking sculpture by Zenos Frudakas. In front is a person in open stride, arms outstretched, face raised toward the sky. Behind this person are four vertical tombs. One is empty—the freed soul has just emerged. In the others, three more beings are coming out. Instantly, I marveled, "What a picture of freedom!" Then I saw the writing in the empty tomb where a head once rested: "Stand here." The artist didn't stop at expressing freedom; he wanted viewers to experience it. I walked into the empty space and stood still. Then I took a delightful step into freedom. Through morning prayer and reflection, we can experience similar meaningful and memorable moments of soulful liberation. Freed persons are the most powerful people on earth.

Human freedom is God's joy. Even when we misuse our freedom, it is not freedom that God condemns but rather its misuse. Put another way, while God may be grieved by what we dream, God is never grieved that we dream. Dreaming is part of what it means to fully experience the divine gift of personhood.

If you can imagine that you have been gifted by God to lead and live your life and recognize that God is your biggest fan, you can more easily give yourself permission to dream other dreams, even expansive ones, that will culminate in your living your divine purpose in grand devotion and delight.

Dreaming Your Desires

In the fourth verse of Psalm 20, David prays, "May [God] grant you your heart's desire, and fulfill all your plans." What a gracious prayer! There are no magical beings who can grant us our heart's desires, but there is the savory truth that we don't have to live with our heartfelt desires always off in the distance. God, the loving Creator of all, cares about our heartfelt desires and, with our help, will bring about their fulfillment.

You may wonder why I say God needs our help. The reason is that you are the only person in all the world who can know your heartfelt desires. I lean toward believing that even God chooses not to know some of our desires and dreams before we have them, opting for holy surprise instead. (Though on the other hand, I have no trouble believing that God is the source of our most compelling and powerful dreams and desires. I envision God saying, "You would be wonderful in many walks of life, but I would almost give a world to see you do thus and so!")

> We don't have to live with our heartfelt desires always off in the distance.

Remember, dreams are often the expressions of our desires. We allow reason to thwart desire. Undaunted and defiantly persistent, desires manifest themselves in our dream life. Identifying and claiming your heart's desires is a critical step in seeing your deep desires blossom in your life. So spend more time listening to your heart and writing down your wholesome, healthy, joy-generating desires. Identify and claim your desires. Look to your heart; listen for the Spirit; notice what others are saying. Most of all, look to your heart. Don't let David's prayer be in vain.

Attending to What Is Alive Inside You

The late singer, pianist, songwriter, and arranger Donny Hathaway is one of my favorite artists. Reared in the black church, Hathaway's music resonates with pathos and passion, suffering and hope. His voice is equally and intensely loyal to both the blues and "blues breakthrough" reality of everyday life. Simply put, Donny Hathaway can make you cry, and he can make you shout for joy.

Hathaway began singing on stage at the age of three with his grandmother, the noted gospel singer Martha Cromwell. The youngster was billed as "Little Donny Pitts, the Nation's Youngest Gospel Singer." The lad was a sensation, but of course, the best was yet to come. In fact, the child prodigy felt something wonderfully amazing welling up inside of him. At age six, Hathaway began telling his grandmother, "You should hear the music I'm hearing in my head."

What would have happened if Hathaway had been unable to hear the music? What if he had heard the music and not noticed, ignored it, or denied it? For countless others to be blessed by the artistry of Donny Hathaway, he had to first honor and trust what was coming to life—the dream music—inside of him.

Dialoguing with Your Desires

Even though I started out early, I was going to be late. Either my directions were wrong, or I had missed a turn. As I continued to drive, I began to feel distraught about not meeting a long-standing commitment, one I dearly wanted to fulfill. In my hopelessness, I uttered a prayer that was part blame and part request. What happened next was most remarkable. I glanced at my directions, received new clarity, reversed direction, saw a sign that pointed me toward my destination, and arrived right on time.

I attribute my small miracle to a mysterious dance of knowledge, desire, and God's grace. Without minimizing the map's guidance and Our Great Guide, I am thinking mostly in this moment of my desire. I really wanted to make it to that event. Indeed, the thought of not being there grieved me.

My memory of what occurred impresses on me the importance of our desires. Is it possible that earnest desire ignites deeper knowing and invites divine blessing? Divine blessing may not be the way you are used to thinking about desire. Many of us grow up disconnecting God and desire. Desires are seen as worldly, often sexual, passions that are hindrances to authentic spirituality. With such thinking deeply entrenched within us, we often dismiss our desires without realizing it. If we do notice them, sometimes it's without giving them a full hearing, fearing the pleasure they produce. After all, how can something so pleasurable be spiritual? We are challenged to see God, spirituality, and pleasure as being integrally connected. Your true pleasure is never far from God's good will for your life. This is the essence of sanctified, delighted spirituality. Authentic fulfilling purpose is rooted in such.

By the way, the word *desire* comes from the Latin *de sidus*, which literally means "from a star." So to dialogue with desires is to reach for the stars and accept inspiration from the heavens. Begin dialoguing with your desires. What do you want? Why do you want it? Can you imagine God blessing your desires? How can you bless your desires more?

Noticing New Beginnings

Allow me to share with you a journal entry written during a visit to Chicago to attend an annual meeting of the Society of Christian Ethics.

> January 5, 2001
> I am on the 11th floor of Chicago's Hyatt
> Regency Hotel, in a room with a "post card" view
> of a section of downtown Chicago. It is early morn-
> ing. I am watching as the red light on the "Inn of

Chicago" sign a few blocks over goes off and lights
in an office building across the street flicker on.
[Some moments later] City streets that were empty a
few minutes ago are now buzzing with cars and
buses, as if someone, somewhere, just said, "Ready,
set, go!" [Seconds later] The sky is blue and I can see
the sunlight reflected at the peaks of nine tall build-
ings. [A moment later] The sun is touching the flags
swaying in the gentle morning breeze and kissing
the snow-covered ground below.

In this moment, this city—any city—is less a picture
of complex problems and more a picture of new beginnings. Lives, relationships, and organizations all go through
cycles of endings and beginnings. Often we spend too
much of our time fixated on what has ended and not
enough time appreciating what is starting. Notice and note
new beginnings more. Trust them more; follow them more.
Pay attention to new ideas that you have about things to do
and avenues to take. Carry a journal or tape recorder to help
you remember a fleeting notion that must be caught and
held in order for it to reveal its full meaning. If you do not
take responsibility for remembering passing thoughts, they
will take their diamonds of new direction with them.

Noticing new beginnings has its share of pain. It is the
pain of seeing less of what we have become familiar with.
Here Judith Viorst, author of *Necessary Losses*, is a helpful guide:
"Throughout our life we grow by giving up. We give up
some of our deepest attachments to others. We give up certain cherished parts of ourselves. . . . Passionate investment

leaves us vulnerable to loss. And sometimes, no matter how clever we are, we must lose."

Dreaming and Wandering

Jimmy Scott is a diminutive, high-voiced saint of a singer who was admired by icons such as Billie Holiday, Marvin Gaye, and Ray Charles. Learning about Jimmy Scott's struggles, sorrows, and joys has made his voice even more sacred to me. Scott sings each note like it's the last one he will ever sing. This relentless attentiveness makes for the slowest, most wondrous singing you will ever hear. My favorite passages in a biography about him, *Faith in Time*, are reflections on Scott's signature singing pace. Jazz critic David Newman observes, "He's the one singer who seems to create space, or expand space. By being so kicked back, he pushes the limits and lets you linger in a way that new ideas have time to develop. As a musician, he allows for miracles." Writer Joel Dorn says of Scott, "Give him all the time and space in the world, and he'll create a new world for you." For his part, Jimmy Scott said he appreciated musical compositions that let him "wander."

Don't force your dreams. Give yourself time and space for wondering and wandering. You can wander in a number of ways. Allot time each day for pondering and reflection. Take "well days" off, days you use to slow down and reflect on who you are and who you are becoming, on where you are and where you are going. Begin writing more about your dreams in your regular journal, or start a new journal just for dreaming and desiring. These are just three ways to wander and wonder on purpose. Can you think of more?

Dream Whispers

A bookstore in the Charlotte, North Carolina, airport has interesting quotes prominently displayed on its walls. One quote held my attention for several minutes. I walked away, but not far before I was drawn back to it. Here is the quote from Logan Pearsall Smith: "What I like in a good author is not what he says but what he whispers."

Take a moment to reflect on some of the things you have heard whispered in your lifetime and some of the things you have whispered. Perhaps it was something you wanted only a single person to hear. Maybe you whispered because you were in a public place and you didn't want to disturb anyone. Perhaps you whispered to yourself because you didn't want to be caught talking to yourself. Do you have such softly spoken words in mind? Now, ask yourself this question: "How important were these whispered words to me at the time I heard or spoke them?"

Of all of life's whispers, some of the most important are the soft, hard words of encouragement we say to ourselves in times of struggle: "I can do this." "I am going to be fine." "Things are going to work out." Sometimes a new calling or a new vision of an old one may whisper its possibility in our life. It does not shout for fear it may alarm you. Live on whisper alert. Pay attention to words you say and hear at lower volumes. Take the time to write down some of what you hear. Note the wisdom of your whispers as they relate to your dreams and aspirations.

You need be on whisper alert for another reason: to access the magnificent insight generator of stillness. Stillness is incomparably consistent when it comes to facilitating deeper awareness and new insight. Stillness necessarily lowers the volume of communication. What you hear about purpose in stillness will not be shouted; it will be wondrously whispered.

Running Past Your Dreams

In my book *Rest in the Storm: Self-Care Strategies for Clergy and Other Caregivers*, I relay the following story about the musk deer of North India. "In the springtime, the roe is haunted by the odor of musk. He runs wildly over hill and ravine with his nostrils dilating and his little body throbbing with desire, sure that around the next clump of trees or bush he will find musk, the object of his quest. Then at last he falls, exhausted, with his little head resting on his tiny hoofs, only to discover that the odor of musk is in his own hide."

It is possible to miss and dismiss the deep wisdom of our dreams by speeded-up living. As you slow down, stop, and feel your life more, you are more likely to sense, feel, and honor your deepest dreams.

Dreaming, Not Sleepwalking

In his classic book on racial oppression, *Invisible Man*, Ralph Ellison refers to persons who practice racial hate and prejudice as "sleeping ones." Ellison warns that "there are few things in the world as dangerous as sleepwalkers." In his fascinating book *Awareness*, Anthony De Mello refers to spirituality as "waking up." His advice on being awake in life—more entirely alive—is profound and worth remembering: "In order to wake up, the one thing you need the most is not energy, or strength, or youthfulness, or even great intelligence. The one thing you need most of all is the readiness to learn something new."

If we are to regularly create and notice new desires and dreams, we must cultivate our capacity for newness. You can do this by being alert to new ideas and more mindful of how your mind has changed about matters. Newness is cultivated through reading outside our favorite genres and regularly initiating conversations with people who are different. We stretch our capacity for newness by beginning new projects that challenge us with different questions and prospects. Newness ought not be ignored or left to chance; we may cultivate it. Otherwise we run the risk of walking in a sleeplike state we mistake for genuinely living.

Loving What You Love

If you have read everything to this point, you know that Jovonna, our youngest child, is one of my best teachers. I have had to cultivate a ready ear for her teachings because they can come at any place and at any time. She doesn't take long, and she seems totally unaware of the weight of her profundity (not bad traits for any teacher to have). As an educator, she has something else going for her: Some of her best lessons are not in her direct pronouncements but rather in the responses she prompts by something she's said.

For example, we were driving along to school one morning and out of the blue she told me, "I like sports." She went on to explain, "I have a friend who doesn't like sports, and she says that it's because she's a girl and girls aren't supposed to like sports. [Pause] But I have another friend and we don't just like sports, we *love* sports. And we're girls." [Pause—never interrupt a good teacher in mid-stride.] "Well, sometimes I agree with my friends just to agree with them, but this time I am not agreeing. I am a girl; I love sports; that's just the way it is." "Well, Jo-Jo," I said (Jo-Jo is Jovanna's nickname), "I think you're right." We pulled up to the school and my teacher ran off, but her words remained.

My daughter made me think about how important it is to know what you love—to name it and own it. In a world of endless choices, it's easy to busy ourselves with a multitude of likes, interests, and curiosities. With all due respect to likes, we need some loves. Moreover, I thought about Jo-Jo's determined choice to love what she loved, even though it meant going against what one of her friends believed about girls and sports. Though Jo-Jo didn't phrase it in this way, she was willing to side with her love against conformity. How many of us have given up dearly loved pursuits, dreams, and ambitions because of the reticence, indifference, and outright rejection of others? Know what you love, and love it, until it, not your fears or the fears of others, gives you good reason to do otherwise.

Speaking of fear, you'll need to work at evicting it or living as if it has been evicted from your life, if you will freely love what you love and live your divine purpose. Fear shrinks us before delightful dreams and ambitions, so much so that we begin to tremble and let possibilities pass us by. Fear keeps us from knowing all we can, showing all we are, and growing expansively into the free, flourishing persons God made us to be and become. Stop letting fear run and ruin your life. Toss it out! Just tell it to leave! Be bold in your banishing. Evict fear daily until its status as an unwanted, uninvited freeloader in your life is made perfectly clear.

Dreams: Our Purpose-Guides

One night, I had three successive dreams that combined to offer a breakthrough I shall never forget. In the first dream, I was seated with someone in a car outside a building. Soon I saw an elderly male emerge. His face showed that he had lived a very long time and a very long time ago. As I continued to look at the man, I sensed that I had seen him before. Suddenly, I connected him to having been a contemporary of my great-grandparents, Peter and Elizabeth Fields. The realization enlivened me. Gleefully, I spoke up. Referring to my brothers, I started reminding the man of "the four little boys" who had visited my grandparents. His demeanor indicated that he didn't need any coaxing or convincing; he knew who I was. Who was this man, in fact? Why did I see him in my dream? What was this dream trying to tell me? What is it trying to tell me still? Upon reflecting on the dream, I wrote in my journal:

> The past comes calling
> Past matters
> Ah, what was!
> Deeply moved
> Move on!

In the second dream, I was standing with someone outside a small house I felt compelled to enter. The camera in the dream focused on a key I held in my hand. How I came to have the key, I do not know. Placing the key into the lock, I opened the door. I entered a museum of a room that appeared to be unlived in. The dream ended. Was I to inhabit this room? Was it enough to notice the room and keep moving? What did the room represent? What did I see? What didn't I see? I reflected:

> New opportunities make their offering to us.
> We make our offerings, or not, to new opportunities.
> Where there is no life, three choices confront us:
> Abide in lifelessness, make life, or
> Move on!

In the third and final dream, I remember being with someone beside a small boat. We dislodged the boat, pushed it toward the water, and got in. We came upon a new shore. I protested that the new place did not appear to be the desired destination. The person with me did not argue. We turned the boat around and started back. As we approached our original starting place, two more paths were open before us. The dream ended before I could choose a new direction. Was the journey taken in the dream a mistake? Do all journeys matter, no matter where they take us? Do all choices matter? Is any choice completely right or totally wrong? I wrote:

> How faithful is it to turn back
> because the land ahead
> looms unfamiliar?
> Move on!

I notice a comforting, common denominator about the dreams: In each of them I was accompanied; I was never alone.

> No, never alone.
> No, never alone.
> Move on!

Dream Again

Sometimes dreams seem to die inside of us. What do we do then? When I asked the question once, this is what I heard:

What do you do
when your dreams
are blown away?
Cry and be still,
and when you are ready
dream again.
Now don't
be afraid
of new dreams
New dreams
have a right to be different,
bolder, riskier.
But befriend them,
host them in your heart.
Embrace them, but not too hard.
The best dreams are soft,
in order to more readily reshape,
if life should blow them away.

Dreams: The Certain Path to Purpose

More than thinking our way to purpose, we desire and
dream our way to purpose. Any thought about your vocation that is not endorsed by your deep desires and dreams
will ultimately leave you empty inside. So give yourself permission to desire and dream with all that you have in you.
Dare to dream. Our best dreams are the ones that challenge
and broaden us the most. I love the following acrostic

developed by Rhonda Myers, one of my former students at Andover Newton Theological School. She conceived DARING as standing for

Dance Across Reluctance; Invite New Growth

Be daring with dreams that inspire you so, they can't help but bless others and please God.

EXERCISES

1. Use the following sentence starters to excavate your desires and jump-start your dreams.

Give yourself permission to desire and dream with all that you have in you.

What I really want is . . .

It would be fun to . . .

If I had $15 million in the bank and just ten years to live, I would . . .

As a child, when people asked me what I wanted to be when I grew up, I told them . . .

I believe I can best serve the world by . . .

My best offering to God, the world, and others is . . .

I most enjoy giving . . .

The things that I do that seem to inspire the most gratitude and joy in people are . . .

2. Name your fears. Write an eviction notice for each one.

9

joyfully playing your dreams

I am writing in a hotel room in Cleveland across the street from a small construction site. I count ten or so workers on this Saturday morning. One man dressed in blue jeans and a white shirt appears to be making adjustments to a doorway. Two others are attaching pieces to or removing pieces from the roof. Several more are just standing around talking. The person that I am most observing is operating a machine that digs a large hole in the ground. The machine has two extensions: a plow similar to the one that drivers use to clear the snow in Massachusetts and an armlike apparatus that breaks at the elbow. It is a big elongated portable shovel. The machine operator is alternating using the two extensions. Indeed, as I watch him now, I believe I have caught his method. He is using the arm to dig the hole and the plow-like feature to move the dirt away.

I am wondering something about these strangers across the street, the machine operator in particular. I wonder if they are having fun. What is he feeling as the ground is breaking? How does it feel to manipulate the contraptions of the machine? Is there a sense of fanciful accomplishment as the worker sees and feels the hole getting deeper and wider? Is there a feeling of excitement to participate in making something new and different? At points, does the worker reminisce about times when he played make-believe, guiding toy machines in the sand? Did he always like dirt or enjoy playing in the dirt? How many persons over there are having fun? How many will experience a sense of play sometime before they leave their work this Saturday morning, a time for cartoon watching and game playing for children around the world, including, perhaps, those in the homes they left a few hours ago in order to be doing what they're doing across the street right now?

Some people would fault my wondering, reminding me that the intent of these workers when they left home was not to go to play but to go to work. Whether are not they are having fun is beside the point. The point is that they do the job they were contracted to do as efficiently as possible. I object. I object to any perspective that strips labor of play. Ideally, if the workers across the street are there because they love breaking, building, and making, they are having as much fun as their children are having at home.

I believe that fun and playfulness are essential attributes of a good or right purpose, a fulfilling purpose, a godly

If you can't play your purpose, it's not your true purpose.

purpose. When it comes to perceiving and practicing purpose, the pleasure element is usually diminished in favor of income prospects, status, and the value of the work to society. Yet if you are earning a good salary, are highly esteemed for the work you do in the world, and are helping humanity in visibly important ways and are not experiencing palpable joy doing what you do, I would suggest that you reconsider your vocational choice. If you can't play your purpose, it's not your true purpose.

The Spirit of Play

One of the most important things we can do as we practice discerning "the will of God" is put some play (flexibility, fun, and faith) into it. Remember, Jesus' vocational pursuits involved wedding feasts, walks by the side of the sea (and sometimes on it), grand picnics, and talking with men in trees, women by wells, and children playing on his knee. Vocation, work, purpose can become too heavy. Vocational discernment and practice do not have to be agonizing or burdensome. Play helps us keep a joyful, creative perspective about life's purpose. Play allows for an attitude of engaging our desires, callings, and perceived obligations with joyful enthusiasm.

There is an ancient Sanskrit word, *lila*, that expresses my meaning perfectly. Richer than our word *play*, *lila* describes divine play, the play of creation, destruction, and re-creation, the folding and unfolding of the cosmos. *Lila*, free and deep, is both the delight and enjoyment of this moment and the play of God. It also means love.

As children, most of us engaged life for the sheer joy and delight of it. Our calling was to play and play some more. Then something happened: We grew up. We began thinking that there was another more important and more serious reason for life. We allowed others to make us feel guilty about our playful desires and pursuits. We traded passionate play for acceptance, seriousness, and power over others. But it doesn't have to continue that way. We can think more playfully about life in general and vocation in particular.

Vocation is something to play with, to create, to shape, mold, configure, and reconfigure in divine play with God. Vocational discernment is not supposed to be a misery-maker but a joy-maker. Vocational clarity and excitement are connected to our being able to play again, to engage life as a delightful, spirited affair.

Play offers a depth of riches. Margaret Guenther describes play as total engrossment in a moment of time-lessness. When we are truly playful, we lose all sense of time; eternity has us, and for the magical moment, nothing else matters. "Play exists for its own sake," she points out.

"Play is for the moment; it is not hurried, even when the pace is fast and timing seems important. When we play, we also celebrate holy uselessness. Like the calf frolicking in the meadow, we need no pretense or excuses. Work is productive; play, in its disinterestedness and self-forgetting, can be fruitful."

> When we are truly playful, we lose all sense of time; eternity has us, and for the magical moment, nothing else matters.

Ted Loder pinpoints the genius of play in its power to make us laugh and thereby set us free. "Laughter is a holy thing. It is as sacred as music and silence and solemnity, maybe more sacred. Laughter is like a prayer, like a bridge over which creatures tiptoe to meet each other. Laughter is like mercy; it heals. When you laugh at yourself, you are free."

Michele Cassou and Stewart Cubley highlight yet another blessing of play, its manner of facilitating the free sounding of our inner voice: "To play is to listen to the imperative inner force that wants to take form and be acted out without reason. It is the joyful, spontaneous expression of one's self. The inner force materializes in the feeling and perception without planning or effort. That is what play is."

Finally, Peter Nachmanovitch speaks majestically of play's enchanting power:

> In play we manifest fresh, interactive ways of relating with people, animals, things, ideas, images, our-

selves. . . . We toss together elements that were for-
merly separate. Our actions take on novel sequences.
To play is to free ourselves from arbitrary restrictions and expand our field of action. Our play fos-
ters richness of response and adaptive flexibility. This
is the evolutionary value of play—play makes us
flexible. By reinterpreting reality and begetting nov-
elty, we keep from becoming rigid. Play enables us
to rearrange our capacities and our very identity so
that we can be used in unforeseen ways.

This final step in living your divine purpose is as vital
as the previous four. Not engaging your purpose in a spirit
of free, open playfulness will nullify the power of your new
liberating beliefs about God, purpose, creativity, and the
spiritual power of imagining or dreaming. Such things are
the vehicles of new belief, necessary for travel. Play is the
fuel that will make your trip worthwhile.

Just how might you expect to be playful in realizing
your vocational dreams? The ways are endless and unique to
each individual. Yet I foresee crucial forms of common play
that we all must engage in if we are to soar vocationally.

Play Enthusiasm

If you have children or nieces and nephews, chances are
you have attended your share of elementary school plays. In
2005, I witnessed the best school play I've ever seen. *The
Audition*, presented by our daughter's sixth-grade class,

was thoughtful, funny, and finely acted. Proof of its power was our watching it for two hours in a hot room and clapping wildly when it was over. After the performance, I asked our little star, Jovonna, how they were able to do so well. She felt that their success had something to do with a cast ritual.

Before each performance, their teacher called them all into a circle and had them assume a squatting position. Next, they were directed to slowly rise, all the while chanting with increasing vigor and volume, "Fun, fun, fun!" When all were standing and after having shouted "fun" for the umpteenth time, the teacher shouted, "Are we ready to do this?" You can guess the answer. Those young actresses and actors stirred up enthusiasm before each presentation. They were on fire for each performance because they chose to be and took time to fire themselves up. Based on the root meaning of *enthusiasm*, such an experience is deeply spiritual. *Enthusiasm* comes from the Greek *en* ("in") and *theos* ("God"). Thus to be filled with enthusiasm is to be in God and to have God in you.

> To be filled with enthusiasm is to be in God and to have God in you.

The Reverend Peter Gomes, dean of chapel at Harvard University, possesses a free and winsome personality. When he is asked, "How are you?" he told me, he resists uttering the standard "I'm OK" or "Fine, thank you." Instead, Rev. Gomes often answers back, "I flourish!" Freedom will do that for you—allow you to grow well, to prosper, to thrive, to flourish. Can you claim this for yourself in the days and weeks ahead? Can you envision yourself enthusiastically flourishing in every dimension of your life?

Play Focus

Chapter 10 of Luke's gospel concludes with an incident involving two sisters and a house guest. Tension arises when one sister, Martha, notices that the other sister, Mary, is AWOL regarding work that needs to be done. While Martha is busy with table and food arrangements, Mary is doing absolutely nothing. Nothing, that is, but sitting at the feet of their guest and listening, like she hasn't a responsibility in the world. I imagine Martha "accidentally" bumping Mary a few times to nudge her into action, but words, stares, and even nudges fail; Mary doesn't move. Finally, Martha decides to go to the source of Mary's lapse, the guest, Jesus. She says, "Tell Mary to help me," perhaps adding, "or both of you will end up at the diner down the street." Jesus responds by telling Martha, "You are worried and distract-ed about many things; there is need of only one thing. Mary has chosen the better part." That having been said, it sounds like the neighborhood diner did have two additional cus-tomers. How dare Jesus take Mary's side?

In fact, Jesus is on Martha's and our side with his words challenging our way of worrying about many things instead of focusing on one thing at a time. Please note, the problem wasn't Martha's concern for the "material" as opposed to Mary's concern for the "spiritual." Hospitality, Martha's work, was spiritual. No, the problem was Martha's paying attention to too many things at once. Mary's strength was her singular focus.

> In a world overflowing with choices, distractions, and tensions, single-mindedness is an unsung skill worth lauding and living.

In a world overflowing with choices, distractions, and tensions, single-mindedness, the ability to attend fully to the matter at hand, is an unsung skill worth lauding and living. When it comes to our purpose, resist the mind-flood. Focus on one or two primary callings at a time. You are never called to do so many tasks that you are unable to do any of them well.

Play Freshness

I wondered if he would be "mailing it in." I've heard the expression used in reference to star entertainers who simply go through the motions of a performance without giving fully and truly of themselves. This past Saturday, the headliner and final act at the Newport Jazz Festival was George Benson, a gifted guitarist and vocalist; he can astound you with either gift. But he's been at it awhile, some thirty or forty years. So as I awaited his appearance, my anticipation was restrained somewhat by my suspicion. As it turned out, Benson did mail in his performance—special delivery.

I focused my binoculars on him the moment he appeared on stage. Only toward the end of his set did I get around to taking the binoculars away from my eyes so that I could clap and sway to the music. Until then, I couldn't shake what I was seeing through the binoculars. Benson was singing and playing with the vitality of someone attempting to win his first Grammy as opposed to someone who has eight of them on his mantle. His playing was particularly powerful for me. There was an intense joy about it—and searching. His facial contortions and animations seemed those of a person seeking to play notes and combinations of notes that he had never played before. He was on a new adventure with his guitar, an instrument he had played thousands of times before. I marveled that he could be so fresh with something so familiar.

Benson's performance impressed upon me that freshness and familiarity are not antonyms. It is possible to experience new vibrancy with tenured reality. The key may be maintaining a learning disposition. Relationships and vocations do not grow stale with time; they grow stale from an inability to imagine a greater depth.

Play Your Personal Integrity

Where were you when you heard that Rosa Parks had died? What were you doing? How did you respond to the news? Though I had not spoken her name or thought about her recently, I found myself momentarily numbed by the news of her passing. It was as if something precious beyond comprehension had left our world, had left me. So I stopped what I was doing and just sat. We rush everything these days, including our grieving. Let us resist moving past the death of Rosa Parks too swiftly. In tribute to someone whose sitting down changed a nation, we would all do well to sit and think.

We rush everything these days, including our grieving. Let us resist moving past the death of Rosa Parks too swiftly.

In her book *Black Womanist Ethics*, Katie Cannon writes about "unshouted courage," calling it "the quality of steadfastness, akin to fortitude, in the face of formidable oppression." Rosa Parks personified "unshouted courage" in her unpretentious act of civil disobedience on a Montgomery, Alabama, bus half a century ago and the calm, deliberate manner in which she recalled her act in countless interviews thereafter. What a stunning contrast to Martin Luther King Jr.'s and Malcolm X's volcanic vocal pronouncements. Rosa Parks reminds us that courage comes in many shapes, sizes, and voices, even a voice just above a whisper. The question is not whether you or I will be courageous like Rosa Parks or any of the sung and unsung champions of the civil rights movement but rather whether we will be true to our convictions in ways that are true to who we are. Will I listen to and own my unique courageous voice? Will you?

I cannot think of Rosa Parks without recalling some of the most profound words I have read concerning her. In *Let Your Life Speak*, Parker Palmer interprets Parks's protest as an action affirming personal wholeness: She refused to think free yet act oppressed. Palmer ponders, "Where do people find the courage to live divided no more when they know they will be punished for it? They have come to understand that no punishment anyone might inflict on them could possibly be worse than the punishment they inflict on themselves by conspiring in their own diminishment."

We conspire in our own diminishment each time we act contrary to our most honorable and liberating beliefs. We are Rosa Parks each time we have the heart to reject what holds us down and reach for what urges us on. Rosa Parks did not have a monopoly on living with integrity; we can do so each day in our aspirations, relationships, and decisions.

Early in her writing career, Alice Walker was asked by a leading national magazine to write about growing up in the South. Though Walker was pleased with what she produced, the magazine suggested major revisions. Walker refused. In a showdown meeting, Walker was informed that she didn't understand, the piece would have to be changed or it would not be published. After considering the positive impact such an article would have on her budding career and weighing that against her integrity as a writer, Walker responded, "It's you who do not understand. All I have to do in life is save my soul." Rosa Parks's decision was a matter of soul-saving: her own and the soul of a nation.

Now, we must be careful that we do not do with Rosa Parks what we do with many of our heroes. We tend to place laudable figures so high on the pedestal of praise that they become untouchable, out of living range. The lessons of Rosa Parks are much too valuable to be stored away in history books and museums. We need her beacon of personal uniqueness and wholeness nearby to behold and manifest in everyday life. In this way, Rosa Parks will not simply be a wondrous woman of saintly dignity and sacred defiance who lived *once* but a spirit of freedom, justice, and personal integrity who lives *now* in each of us.

Play Joy

Our eldest daughter, Jasmine Karla, was born on Thanksgiving Day. From the beginning, she was a bright ball of energy with the widest eyes you have ever seen. Because she was naturally ebullient, whenever she became sad about anything, it was heart-wrenching for me. One day, when she was five or six years old, she was down about something. I took her in my arms and before I knew it, a song came out. I made it up as I went along, both the lyrics and the melody. To my knowledge, I had never thought or mouthed it before until that moment. What is now known as "Jazzy's Blues Song" is best heard. The highs and drops of the voice adds immeasurably to these simple lyrics:

> Don't cry, Jazzy.
> The sun's about to shine, Jazzy.
> Don't be sad, Jazzy.
> Be glad, Jazzy.

On the last syllable, my voice goes higher and higher, out of my range to the point of my bearing barely able to sound the note. The strained high-sounding ending almost always evokes laughter from Jasmine, now in her early twenties. You may recall a silly song or two that you once created to mend a broken heart. More important than the song was the sentiment behind it: We wanted our loved one to have joy, to smile, to be happy, to exhibit a fanciful and fun-filled freeness toward life. Sure, people will be sad. But our will is that sadness not become the norm; the norm is joy. If we can feel this way about our loved ones and their experience with life, how much more does God feel this way about us and our experience with life? Your joyfulness matters to God.

When it comes to seeking purpose, what God has already said matters just as much as what God is saying. And what God has already said and offers through the person and expressions of Jesus is "life more abundantly." No true and honest vocational undertaking in pursuit of the abundant life is outside the will of God. Can you believe that

> Can you believe that what God wants most from your life is for you to have the time of your life?

abundance includes joy, pleasure, fun, and playfulness? Will you give yourself permission to cocreate a living purpose that makes you feel happy and allows you to have faithful fun? Can you believe that what God wants most from your life is for you to have the time of your life? God wants you to have the time of your life in your leisure, in your relationships, and in the area that draws so much of your time and energy, your work.

You Were Born to Play and Soar

I believe that we were all born to play and soar, to experience amazing joy and achievement in every dimension of life. Through speaking and writing, I inspire others to embrace their deeper spiritual energy, thereby unleashing new and dynamic creative power. Such empowerment is not limited to the few and the favored. It is the birthright of all of us as children of God. Second Corinthians 3:6 ends with the phrase "but the Spirit gives life." Through our thoughts and actions, we play our life's song. Oliver Wendell Holmes, it is said, insightfully observed, "Most of us go to our graves with our music still inside us." An abundant, creative, delightful life is yours for the playing! You were born to play!

Isaiah 40:31 has a wonderful image of persons "flying like eagles." Too often, we allow negative belief systems that we construct over time to restrict the free flight of wonderful dreams and deeds. Why not aspire and achieve to ever-greater heights in your relationships, your work, and your leisure? You were born to soar! Don't be afraid of God's grand purpose of playful soaring.

Each morning, I take time to be still, receive God's love, embrace my personhood, humanity, and creation, and welcome the day. I have written about this morning ritual in a book called *Morning B.R.E.W.* Visualization is an important aspect of my morning devotion. Sometimes I mentally create the images; sometimes the images seem to create themselves.

One morning, during a vocational transition of my own, I saw myself on a raft. There was darkness all around. Though tense, I allowed myself to stay with the image. In a moment, the tension mounted as I appeared to be coming to a drop. Fascinated by the intensity of the imagery, I allowed myself to fall. Downward I went. In free fall, something wonderful happened; I reversed direction and headed back upward. While ascending, a transformation took place, and I became an eagle. That's right, an eagle. Amazed, I allowed myself to soar, leaning into the experience. Soon after, I heard these words in my mind: "Don't be afraid to fly."

These words set off some sobering reflections. I felt fear in the beginning of the imagery, when I was on the raft. The most fearless moment of all was flying. I felt exhilaration as I soared. Yet the word to me was "Don't be afraid to fly."

As I thought about it, it began to dawn in me that while I enjoyed the fancifulness of adventuring flight, I was afraid of some things that flight meant, including being off the ground of familiarity, moving away from the known, and flying into the unknown. Though I readily enjoyed the soaring, I needed to come to terms with my conscious and unconscious reticence regarding the costs.

Whenever we launch ourselves into new vocational territory, we naturally experience a mixture of euphoria and dread—euphoria because we are filled with the Holy Spirit of exhilarating new life; dread because new life is necessarily wrought with the risks of the unknown. Naming the dread somehow makes it less dreadful.

While thrilling, flying involves being off the ground of the known. Flying takes us places we have never been before.

May you live with playful purpose and lighthearted intention. Know this: Whatever path you choose, God is with you.

EXERCISES

1. Remember and then describe your play-life as a child. What did you enjoy doing? How did you have the most fun?

2. Identify the "fun factor" in past vocations and vocations you are considering.
3. Identify tasks and skills that have brought you joy in life. What still brings joy?
4. Finish this thought: "It would be fun to . . ."
5. What could you do to make God smile?
6. How do you imagine yourself bringing real joy to others? To the world?

notes

Preface

p. ix: Anthony De Mello, *Awareness: A De Mello Spirituality Conference in His Own Words* (New York: Doubleday, 1990), p. 29.

Chapter One: The Tyranny and Triumph of Choosing

p. 2: Lyrics from "Expect Your Miracle" by Ebernita "Twinkie" Clark, © Bridgeport Music BMI.

p. 13: Madeleine L'Engle, *Glimpses of Grace: Daily Thoughts and Reflections* (San Francisco: HarperSanFrancisco, 1996), p. 34.

Chapter Two: The Anatomy of Stuckness

p. 16: De Mello, *Awareness*, p. 29.

p. 18: Barry Schwartz, *The Paradox of Choice: Why More Is Less* (New York: HarperCollins, 2004), p. 2.

p. 19: David Whyte, *Crossing the Unknown Sea: Work as a Pilgrimage of Identity* (New York: Riverhead Books, 2001), pp. 123, 133.

p. 21: Martin Luther King Jr., "Letter from Birmingham Jail," April 16, 1963.

Chapter Three: The Divine Adventure

p. 32: John Ayto, *Dictionary of Word Origins* (New York: Arcade, 1991).

p. 34: Rick Warren, *The Purpose Driven Life: What on Earth Am I Here For?* (Grand Rapids, Mich.: Zondervan, 2002).

Chapter Four: Our Great Beloved Partner

p. 47: Gregg Levoy, *Callings: Finding and Following an Authentic Life* (New York: Three Rivers Press, 1997), p. 53.

p. 56: Sue Monk Kidd, *The Secret Life of Bees* (New York: Viking Penguin, 2002), p. 288.

p. 58: Kirk Byron Jones, *Rest in the Storm: Self-Care Strategies for Clergy and Other Caregivers* (Valley Forge, Pa.: Judson Press), pp. 125–126.

Chapter Five: The Wild Thrill of Wide-Open Possibility

p. 66: Brenda Ueland, *If You Want to Write*, 2nd ed. (Saint Paul, Minn.: Graywolf Press, 1987), p. 50.

p. 67: Henri J. M. Nouwen, *Bread for the Journey* (London: Darton, Longman & Todd, 1996), p. 136.

pp. 86–87: Philip Moffitt, in Guy Kawasaki, *Hindsights: The Wisdom and Breakthroughs of Remarkable People* (Hillsboro, Ore.: Beyond Words, 1994), p. 64.

pp. 87–88: Hokusai, in Robert Fulghum, *Words I Wish I Wrote: A Collection of Writing That Inspired My Ideas* (New York: HarperCollins, 1999), p. 55.

p. 94: Donald Hall, *Life Work* (Boston: Beacon Press, 1993), p. 41.

p. 94: Benny Golson, in Lewis Porter, *John Coltrane: His Life and Music* (Ann Arbor: University of Michigan Press, 1998), p. 36.

pp. 96–97: Mark Twain, letter to George Bainton, October 15, 1888.

Chapter Six: Not Just Creature but Creator

pp. 107–108: Jennifer Ebert, "Business Unorthodox: Creativity and the Bottom Line," 2002 [http://www.lookatmorestuff.com/Play Exe.pdf], p. 1.

p. 109: Richard Florida, *The Rise of the Creative Class* (New York: Basic Books, 2002), p. 8.

pp. 110–111: Carolyn Dell'uomo, "The Shaman of Creativity: An

Interview with Hal Zina Bennett," 2005 [http://www.halzinaben nett.com/interview.htm].

pp. 111–112: Hal Zina Bennett, ibid.

p. 112: Gordon D. Kaufman, *In the Beginning . . . Creativity* (Minneapolis, Minn.: Augsburg Fortress, 2004).

Chapter Seven: Three Great Creative Powers

p. 122: Viktor E. Frankl, *Man's Search for Meaning* (Boston: Beacon Press, 1959), p. 86.

p. 123: Kirk Byron Jones, *Addicted to Hurry: Spiritual Strategies for Slowing Down* (Valley Forge, Pa.: Judson Press, 2003), p. 116.

pp. 129–130: Oriah Mountain Dreamer, *What We Ache For: Creativity and the Unfolding of Your Soul* (New York: HarperCollins, 2005), p. 128.

p. 130: Herbie Hancock, *Head Hunters* [album notes], Sony, 1997.

p. 131: Herbert Benson and William Proctor, *The Breakout Principle: How to Activate the Natural Trigger That Maximizes Creativity, Athletic Performance, Productivity, and Personal Well-Being* (New York: Scribner, 2003), pp. 58–59.

pp. 132–133: Gene Bartlett, *Postscript to Preaching: After Forty Years, How Will I Preach Today?* (Valley Forge, Pa.: Judson Press, 1981), p. 80.

pp. 133–134: Diane Wolkstein, "Beyond Views: An Exchange with Thich Nhat Hanh," *Parabola*, Winter 2005, p. 21.

p. 134: Mary Oliver, "Luna," *Why I Wake Early* (Boston: Beacon Press, 2004), p. 41.

p. 135: Zora Neale Hurston, in Valerie Boyd, *Wrapped in Rainbows: The Life of Zora Neale Hurston* (New York: Scribner, 2003), p. 87.

p. 137: Stephen King, *On Writing: A Memoir of the Craft* (New York: Scribner, 2000), p. 153.

Chapter Eight: Dreaming Your Way to Purpose

p. 143: Kahlil Gibran, *The Beloved: Reflections on the Path of the Heart* (New York: Penguin, 1997), p. 25.

p. 143: Howard Thurman, *Deep Is the Hunger* (New York: HarperCollins, 1951), p. 47.

pp. 151–152: Judith Viorst, *Necessary Losses: The Loves, Illusions, Dependencies, and Impossible Expectations That All of Us Have to Give Up in Order to Grow* (New York: Free Press, 2002), p. 16.

p. 152: David Newman and Joel Dorn are quoted in Jimmy Ritz, *Faith in Time: The Life of Jimmy Scott* (New York: Da Capo, 2002), pp. 155 and 165.

p. 153: Logan Pearsall Smith, *All Trivia: Trivia, More Trivia, Afterthoughts, Last Words* (New York: Harcourt Brace, 1934).

p. 154: Jones, *Rest in the Storm*, p. 51.

p. 155: Ralph Ellison, *Invisible Man* (New York: Random House, 1952), p. 5.

p. 155: De Mello, *Awareness*, p. 28.

Chapter Nine: Joyfully Playing Your Dreams

pp. 165–166: Margaret Guenther, *Toward Holy Ground: Spiritual Directions for the Second Half of Life* (Cambridge, Mass.: Cowley, 1995).

p. 166: Ted Loder, "Tickled from Behind," in *Tracks in the Straw: Tales Spun from the Manger*, rev. ed. (Philadelphia: Innisfree Press, 1997), p. 73.

p. 166: Michele Cassou and Stewart Cubley, *Life, Paint, and Passion: Reclaiming the Magic of Spontaneous Expression* (New York: Tarcher, 1996), p. 40.

pp. 166–167: Peter Nachmanovitch, *Free Play: Improvisation in Life and Art* (New York: Tarcher, 1990), p. 43.

p. 172: Katie G. Cannon, *Black Womanist Ethics* (Atlanta, Ga.: Scholars Press, 1988), p. 144.

p. 173: Parker J. Palmer, *Let Your Life Speak: Listening for the Voice of Vocation* (San Francisco: Jossey-Bass, 2000), p. 34.

pp. 173–174: The anecdote about Alice Walker is from Paul Rogat Loeb, *Soul of a Citizen* (New York: St. Martin's/Griffin, 1999), p. 46.

the author

A native of New Orleans, Kirk Byron Jones is the son of Ora Mae Jones and the late Frederick Jesse Jones. He is married to Mary Brown-Jones of Boston, and they are the parents of Jasmine, Jared, Joya, and Jovonna Jones.

Rev. Jones is a graduate of Loyola University and Andover Newton Theological School and holds a Doctor of Ministry degree from Emory University and a Doctor of Philosophy degree from Drew University.

A pastor for twenty-five years, Rev. Jones was the founding minister of Beacon Light Baptist Church in New Orleans and senior minister at Calvary Baptist Church, Chester, Pennsylvania; Ebenezer Baptist Church, Boston; and First Baptist Church, Randolph, Massachusetts.

Throughout his pastoral ministry, Rev. Jones served on various religious and civic committees at the local and national level. He is currently a professor of ethics and preaching at Andover Newton Theological School and serves as guest preacher and teacher at churches, schools, and conferences throughout the United States.

He is the author of six books, and his articles have been published in numerous journals, including *The Christian Century, Leadership, Gospel Today, Pulpit Digest,* and *The African*

American Pulpit, a quarterly preaching journal he cofounded in 1997.

Rev. Jones enjoys family life, reading, listening to music (especially jazz), and having new learning adventures every day.

To learn more about Kirk Byron Jones and spiritual empowerment through play, visit http://www.playand soar.com, http://www.brewseries.com, and http://www. savoringpace.com.

index

A

Acts, Book of, 75–76
Addicted to Hurry: Spiritual Strategies for Slowing Down (Jones), 123
Adult thoughts, about God, 57–58
Advent, 22, 23
Affirmation, need for, 105–106
Akeelah and the Bee (film), 99
Amos 5, 101–102
Awareness (De Mello), 16, 155
Ayto, J., 32–33

B

Bartlett, G., 132–133
Beacon Light Baptist Church, 1–2
Beginnings, new, 150–152
Benefits, of open purpose concept, 89–97
Bennett, H. Z., 111–112
Benson, G., 171
Benson, H., 131–132
Bible, 46–47. *See also* specific books
Black Womanist Ethics (Cannon), 172–173
The Breakout Principle (Benson, Proctor), 131–132
Brock, A., 12
Burnout, and stuckness, 19–20

C

Call, concept of. *See* Purpose; Vocational discernment
Call of God. *See* Purpose; Vocational discernment
Callings: Finding and Following an Authentic Life (Levoy), 47–48
Campbell, J., 144
Cannon, K., 172–173
Cassou, M., 166
Change, 82–83, 92–93
Chaos, and domineering God, 47–48
Childlike thoughts, about God, 57–58
Children of Israel, 22
Choice, 17–19, 121–127
Clown, concept of and God, 59–60
Cocreation with God, and purpose, 120–138
Conformity, vs. love, 155–157
2 Corinthians 3:6, 176
Creative freedom, as gift from God, 35
Creativity: and esteem, 105–106; and fixed purpose concept, 11–12; as gift from God, 35; growing prominence of, 107–111; and open purpose,

91; and purpose, 114–117; and
spirituality, 111–114; ways to
stimulate, 128–137
Cromwell, M., 148
*Crossing the Unknown Sea: Work as a Pil-
grimage of Identity* (Whyte),
19–20
Cubley, S., 166

D
DARING acrostic, 161
Davis, M., 61
De Mello, A., ix, xi, 16, 155
Decision making, 45–46, 124–125
Delight, 12–14, 39–41
Dell'uomo, C., 110–111
Dependency, and view of God,
57–58
Desires, 141–142, 147–150
Dialogue, 50–54, 90–91, 149–150
Dictionary of Word Origins (Ayto),
32–33
Divine appointment, and voca-
tional discernment, 6–10
Divine play (*lila*), 165
Divinity, of dreams, 143–144
Dorn, J., 152
Dreams: attending to, 148–149;
and desires, 141–142,
147–148; divinity of, 143–144;
and excitement, 142–143; and
freedom, 140–141, 146; and
possibilities, 144–145; as pur-
pose-guides, 157–161; vs.
sleepwalking, 155; and wandering, 152–153; and whispers,
153–154. *See also* Imagination

E
E-mail, for author, 29
Ebert, J., 107–108
Ellington, E. K. "Duke", 61, 106,
120
Ellison, R., 155
Empowerment, and creativity, 37
Emptiness, images of, 70–71
Enthusiasm, as form of play,
167–169
Esteem, and creativity, 105–106
Excitement, and dreams, 142–143
Expectations, and creativity, 128–129

F
Faith in Time (Ritz), 152
Faithfulness, concept of, 8, 28–29
Fear, 20–21, 157
Fields, E., 157
Fields, P., 157
Fitzgerald, E., 61
Florida, R., 109
Fo, D., 58–59
Focus, as form of play, 169–170
Frankl, V., 122
Freedom: and concept of God,
58–64; creative, as gift from
God, 35, 48–49; and domineer-
ing God, 46–47; and dreams,
140–141, 146; and embracing
choice, 124–125; and God as
divine parent, 43–44; and God
of dialogue, 50–54; and pursu-
ing vocation, 69–71
Freshness, as form of play,
170–171
Frudakas, Z., 146

G

Gabriel, 52–53

Gethsemane, Garden of, 54

Gibran, K., 143

Glimpses of Grace (L'Engle), 13

God: and childlike thoughts about, 57–58; cocreation with, 114–117; concept of and vocational discernment, 58–64; as creativity, 112–114; of dialogue, 50–54; as divine parent, 43–44; as domineering, 45–50; images of, 59–62; reenvisioning of, 55–57; and waiting, 22–29

God-ness, 80, 105

God's will: and decision making, 124–125; and fixed purpose concept, 10–14; as invitation, 90–91; perception of, 46–47, 49; and purpose, xiv, 77–81; and spirit of play, 164–167; and vocational discernment, 6–10; and waiting on God, 22–29, 37–38

Golson, B., 94

Gomes, P., 168–169

Guenther, M., 165–166

Guidance, divine, 10, 14

H

Hall, D., 94

Hancock, H., 130–131

Hathaway, D., 148–149

Helplessness, unlearning of, 37

Hokusai, 87–88

Holmes, O. W., 176–177

Holy openness, and creativity, 132–134

Holy Spirit, as divine energy, 113

Hudson River experience, 3–10, 39

Hurricane Katrina, 31

Hurston, Z. N., 135

I

If You Want to Write (Ueland), 66–67

Imagination, 86, 91. *See also* Dreams

In the Beginning . . . Creativity (Kaufman), 112

Inevitability, and stuckness, 21–22

Inner voice, and creativity, 130–131

Integrity, as form of play, 172–174

Intel Corporation, 107

Invisible Man (Ellison), 155

Irenaeus, 40

Isaiah 6:8, 68

Isaiah 35:10, 59

Isaiah 40:31, 23, 116, 177

Isaiah 43:19, 126

J

Jacob, 22

Jazz music, 67, 110

Jazz musician image, of God, 61

"Jazzy's Blues Song," 175

Jeremiah 1:5, 5

Jeremiah 31:13, 59

Jesus: ascension of, 75–76; and changing passions, 83–86; as creative personality, 112–113; and God of dialogue, 53–54, 90–91; in Luke 10, 169–170; and power to create choices, 126–127; resurrection of, 85–86; and "sinners,"

103–105; and vision of human possibility, 90

Job transitions, as positive, 92–93

John 16:24, 59

Johnson, G., 1–2

Jones, O. M., 104

Joseph, and Jesus, 84

Joseph, of Old Testament, 22

Journaling, 150–151, 153, 158–159

Joyfulness, 134–136, 174–176

"Just a Closer Walk with Thee" (hymn), 26

K

Kaufman, G., 112

Kidd, S. M., 56

"Killing Us Softly" (lecture), 77

King, Jr., M. L., xii–xiii, 21, 65, 172

King, S., 137

Kingdom of God, as within, 103–104

L

The Last Holiday (film), 144

Latifah, 144

Laughter, 58–59, 166

Leisure, and creativity, 131–132

L'Engle, M., 13

"Let There Be Laughter" (sermon), 58–59

Let Your Life Speak (Palmer), 173

Let's Make a Deal (game show), 20–21

Levoy, G., 47–48

Life-deadening ideas, losing of, 10–14

Life Work (Hall), 94

Lila (divine play), 165

Loder, T., 166

Long, Jr., E., 66

Looking within, and increased clarity, 76

Loss of the known, and stuckness, 16–17

Love: vs. conformity, 155–157; as gift from God, 106; supremacy of, 104; as unconditional, 61–62

Luke 2:10, 59

Luke 4, 53–54

Luke 6:21, 59

Luke 10, 169–170

Luke 24:49, 116

M

Malcolm X, 172

Mandela, N., 134

Man's Search for Meaning (Frankl), 121–122

Martha, in Luke 10, 169–170

Mary (mother of Jesus), 52–53, 90–91

Mary (sister of Martha), in Luke 10, 169–170

Meditation, 70–71

Meekness, 115

Mental stillness, 129–130, 154

Mentoring, 85

Moffitt, P., 86–87

Morning B.R.E.W. (Jones), 177

Moses, and God of dialogue, 50–52, 90–91

Mount Hermon Baptist Church, 27, 72

Multiple-career mindset, 94–95

Myers, R., 161

Mystery, problem of, 25
Myth of singular divine purpose, 71–73

N
Nachmanovitch, P., 166–167
Necessary Losses (Viorst), 151–152
New beginnings, noticing of, 150–152
Newman, D., 152
Newness, capacity for, 155
Nitric oxide, and leisure, 132
Nonanxious dreaming. *See* Dreams
Not-knowingness, sacred, 132–134
Nouwen, H., 67

O
Ocean of unconditional love, as image of God, 61–62
Oliver, M., 134
Options, and power to perceive, 125–126
Oriah Mountain Dreamer, 129–130

P
Palmer, P., 173
Paradox of choice, 18
Parks, R., 172–174
Passion, and purpose, 73–77, 81–86
Pentecost, 113
Play, forms of, 164–174
Playfulness, and creativity, 129, 136–137
"Possibilities book," and dreams, 144–145
Power, and choice, 121–127

Powers, of humans, 115–117
Proctor, W., 131–132
Proverbs 15:13, 59
Proverbs 15:15, 59
Psalm 20, 147
Psalm 23, 46
Psalm 40:1, 23
Purpose: benefits of open concept of, 89–97; beyond success, 86–88; and changing workplace, 82–83; as cocreation with God, 120–138; and concept of call, 50–54; and creativity, 114-115; and cultivating a changing mind, 88–89; dreams as guides to, 157–161; myth about, 71–73; and passion, 73–77, 81–86; and question of God's will, xiv, 77–81; redefining of, 32–37; summary of steps for, 39–41; undoing predetermination of, 67–71. *See also* Vocational discernment
The Purpose-Driven Life (Warren), 34–35

Q
Queen Latifah, 144

R
Rachel, 22
"Reach for Tomorrow" (song), 61
Reflection, time for, 152–153
Rest in the Storm: Self-Care Strategies for Clergy and Other Caregivers (Jones), 58–59, 154
Resurrection, of Jesus, 85–86
Revelation 21:4, 59

S

Sacred incredible, acceptance of, 117–118

Schwartz, B., 18

Scott, J., 61, 152

The Secret Life of Bees (Kidd), 56

Self-debasement, 100–102

Self-denial, 115

Selfhood, valuations of, 100–102

September 11, 2001, 31

Sexism, 77

Shadow, of selfish God, 25–26

Silence, and creativity, 129–130, 154

Singlemindedness, 170

"Sinners," and Jesus, 103–105

Sleepwalking, vs. dreams, 155

Smith, L. P., 153

Spirituality, 111–114, 155

Stillness, and creativity, 129–130, 154

Stress, 19–20

Stuckness: and burnout, 19–20; and fear of wrong choices, 20–21; and inevitability, 21–22; and loss of the known, 16–17; source of, 70; and tyranny of choices, 17–19; and waiting on God, 22–29

Success, purpose beyond, 86–88

Sunday Night Live, 2

T

Tension, creative, 47–48, 49–50

Thich Nhat Hanh, 133–134

Thurman, H., 120–121, 143

2 Timothy 1:7, 116

Twain, M., 96–97

Tyranny, of choices, 17–19

U

Ueland, B., 66–67

Unconditional love, 61–62

V

Viorst, J., 151–152

Visualization, 70–71, 177

Vocational discernment: and concept of God, 58–64; goal of, 6; and God as divine parent, 44; and God's will, 6–10. *See also* Purpose

W

Waiting, on God, 21–29, 37–38

Walker, A., 173–174

Wandering, and dreams, 152–153

Warren, R., 34–35

"Watch Heaven Rejoice" (Jones), 137–138

What We Ache For: Creativity and the Unfolding of the Human Heart (Oriah Mountain Dreamer), 129–130

Whispers, and dreams, 153–154

Whyte, D., 19–20

Will of God. *See* God's will

Williams, M. L., 61

Witness Workshop, 2

Work-joy, 94

Workplace change, 82–83, 92–93

Worship, and human "worthship," 100–102

Y

You-ness, 80